—and everything nice

—and everything nice

A PARENTS' GUIDE TO
BRINGING UP DAUGHTERS

by
VANCE HYDE

Illustrated by CYNTHIA ROCKMORE

DAVID McKAY COMPANY, INC.
New York

TO THE

WISE AND WONDERFUL MAN WHO FATHERED

THE DAUGHTERS AND THE BOOK

Grateful acknowledgment is due Mrs. Doris Rechin, without whose friendship and loyalty—and typewriter—this project might never have been completed.

Grateful acknowledgment is also due *Parents' Magazine,* in which two of the chapters of this book first appeared.

Contents

—and everything nice

CHAPTER 1

Daughters Are for Fun

MOTHERS know about little girls.

They don't always tell, but it's knowledge a woman carries in her blood—that daughters are often more fun for mothers than sons.

Not better.

Not more to be proud of.

Not easier to rear or harder. Just often more fun.

You have to find this out from other mothers; Drs. Spock and Gesell and Ilg and their distinguished colleagues don't include that information in their books. In fact, they take the comfortable attitude that the same rules, the same techniques apply interchangeably for John and Joan. Which just isn't so. Any parent who has both boys and girls can tell you that if you are going to rear your sons and daughters "by the book," you'll need two different books.

That inborn knowledge granted to mothers, that instinct to enjoy our daughters to the hilt, worked without a hitch for years and generations and centuries. It wasn't just the surface joys that meant so much—brushing their silky hair, glorying in frilled nurseries and ruffled pinafores, discovering the old-new magic of clothespin dolls and hollyhock ladies. No, it was something deeper.

A closeness.

Then, all within the span of a few years, they betrayed us— the educators, the psychologists, the writers, the experts in child development. Suddenly, overnight, to have fun with any of our children became suspect, to have fun with our daughter became downright unwholesome.

When we cocked an uneasy ear to the warnings of Freud and Dewey, when we winced under Philip Wylie's merciless caricature of us, something of the joy evaporated from our homes, and without the joy, the burden of responsibility was a weary weight. We had no rights, only duties; no pleasures, only guilt about all the ways in which we might just possibly warp these impressionable young ids.

Poppycock! Of course daughters are for fun. How else could we possibly justify the trouble they are, and the aggravation, and the work? And I have observed that it is *not* the women who enjoy their children unashamedly who are "moms."

No, it is the woman who suddenly realizes that her brood is grown and gone, with never a year of joy to show for all the years of work and worry—that's the mother who will be a typical, clinging, after-all-I've-done-for-you "mom." It's the father who never really knew his child at all who will storm about the house, fuming at the ingratitude of his baby girl wanting to leave her poor old father to go to the big city, or to marry, or indeed wanting to leave him for any reason at all.

Well, there'll be no agony of remorse at our house on *that* account, or even that vague twilight of regret that makes it a heartbreak to see our "babies" grow up.

Before our youngsters were born, we vowed we'd enjoy every day of their childhood, right from the beginning, while they were small and special. Raise 'em right and wish 'em well, that was to be our motto.

But, alas, though the urge to enjoy our children may be in-born, the techniques for accomplishing it do not spring full-blown from race memory, we found. Or perhaps it is only that the crepe-hangers have done their work too well. Whatever the reason, false starts and nagging doubts bedeviled us when our firstborn was quite new, and checking among our friends, we find that we were not alone in that. But we never wavered in our conviction that this was the right goal: that the members of a family should *enjoy* one another.

Eventually we found our way, as all parents do who care enough; now perhaps our trial-and-error discoveries may save other parents a stumble or two on their climb to the same goal.

It's a goal well worth the climb—never doubt it. In the first place, when your approach to child rearing is gay instead of grim, the result is finer children. But it isn't just their child-hoods that you are shaping; you are deciding their futures and their children's futures, too.

The power a parent once wielded through the arranged marriage palls beside the influence the psychologically enlight-ened modern parent can exert. This is particularly true of the influence a mother exerts on her daughters, who look to her for their pattern of womanhood. The kind of man your daugh-ter marries, the kind of wife she will be, the friends she will will choose, the jobs she will hold, her success in every area of living—all these you are deciding now, while she is still in her playpen or riding her first two-wheeler.

But this is only one of the challenges, and joys, of having a little girl. There are so many more.

That is what this book is about—not instructions for rearing children, but ideas, notes, jottings of experiences that have been fun for us and for our three daughters. A sort of chronicle of contentment, a testimony to the unique possibilities for laughter, adventure, and delight that are there for the sharing in any home that is blessed with little girls.

CHAPTER 2

Pretty Is As Pretty Is

WHEN Grandma was a girl, beauty was an accident of birth. If you weren't born beautiful, there was a chant composed to console you, "Pretty is as pretty does." But it was a dubious consolation; then, as now, every realistic woman knew that a good, sweet girl who was pretty had a big advantage over a good, sweet girl who was not.

Today we work at beauty. We realize that by means of discriminating hair styling, consistent complexion care, subtle make-up magic, and clothes wisely chosen to enhance her type, any woman can create the illusion of beauty. Those of us blessed with little girls soon discover that such alchemy can be wrought at an amazingly early age.

At first glance, the adolescent years would seem to be the time for initiation into the feminine world of beauty secrets.

7

And it is true that the traditional self-improvement sessions between a girl and her mirror are terribly important in the life of a teen-ager. For one thing, experimenting with make-up, trying new hair styles, dabbling in a varied palette of nail-polish shades, all provide a release from those vague tensions and restless urges that plague the adolescent.

Also, this is one firm island in the stormy teen years where mother and daughter stand on the common ground of shared interest. As a matter of fact, this is one of the very few areas of living where a daughter is quite apt to know more than her mother, an exhilarating experience for any youngster. If this does happen, if in this one rare instance a teen-ager finds herself in the role of mentor, if her mother is willing to listen and learn and thereby gains a more up-to-date awareness of her own beauty potentials, their whole relationship benefits.

But a girl's preoccupation with her appearance develops long before adolescence. And this early interest provides us with a secret weapon not available to the mothers of little boys: the endless rules of childhood—the washing and brushing, the balanced meals, the hanging up and putting away, the early to bed and early to rise—all these can be presented as the groundwork for beauty, an approach with far greater appeal for any little girl than the time worn "because it's good for you."

One obvious advantage of this right-from-the-beginning emphasis on looks is that it develops a set of completely automatic habits of good grooming. The little girl who is taught to bathe daily, to wash her face gently, thoroughly, and consistently every night of her young life, who is building up fine food habits, will suffer a minimum of teen-age skin problems when she reaches adolescence. The mother who encourages her toddler to join her in a brief exercise session each day, who strengthens her through the years with vitamins and ample sleep and brisk fresh air, who encourages her to join in active sports, who supplies her with dancing lessons and balanced meals and shoes of faultless fit, this mother is doing more to ensure for her daughter a regal carriage and a model's walk than she could hope to accomplish by years of nagging reminders about good posture.

Truly a daughter's beauty training can be considered as beginning almost from the day of her birth. From the morning when she splashes in her first sudsy bath, the first time you fluff up her peach-down fuzz or brush her silky curls around your finger, you are setting the stage for her training toward beauty.

But however desirable it is to establish these patterns early, they could be learned much later, even in young adulthood. Why, then, this urgency, this insistence upon an early start? Because a girl's own evaluation of her attractiveness won't wait. If all through her childhood years she feels like an ugly duckling, then though she may blossom into a lovely young woman her blooming will come too late. She will never really believe in her own good looks.

The little plain jane who hears through all her early years that she is mousy, or scrawny, or isn't-it-a-pity-the-poor-little-thing-had-to-inherit-Jim's-nose, grows up with a hurt so deep it never wholly heals. Eleanor Roosevelt, Elsa Maxwell, Imogene Coca, have told how they still wince, remembering the cruel realization that others found them unappealing.

On the other hand, the little girl who grows up "feeling beautiful," to use the great Ziegfeld's perceptive phrase, is the little girl who grows up serene and confident. In fact, feeling beautiful can change a child's whole personality. Pretty *does* pretty much as pretty *is*, you will discover. And ugly duckling or serene young swan—the responsibility rests squarely upon you while she is small.

Not that you will find advice here on beauty routines. Experts have covered that field far more competently than I could hope to do. But I am going to pass along to you a discovery that I made in the days before full-time motherhood, when the sign on my office door read Fashion Coordinator. I have seen so many children transformed by this simple formula into real beauties that I am convinced that the mother who starts her daughter off this way is giving her a priceless advantage.

The Little Women Formula, we might call it, if we really need a name. For the formula for having a beautiful daughter rests firmly on *dressing to type*, and the four basic types of little girls have never been more dramatically drawn than they were in Jo, Meg, Amy, and Beth, of *Little Women*.

As a fashion counselor I found that the March girls, in that book, are such familiar figures that my mother-and-daughter clients needed no lengthy descriptions to recognize the characteristics of each type. Most children have already identified themselves with one of these little heroines from the past, and dressing by the Little Women Formula appealed to their sense of the dramatic.

Best of all, the names, unlike adjectives, carry no stigma. And that is wise, for a child is never too young to learn that no one type has a monopoly on beauty. Yet for years we lived with the odd conception that only the pretty-pretty Amy Marches were worthy of homage. Perhaps it was Shirley Temple who started it—surely there has never been a child more pure Amy than Shirley Temple. Whatever the reason, curls became required equipment for everyone's daughter, and designers turned out flounced, be-ruffled dresses with a nation of Amy's in mind.

But not today! Now our stores are stocked with a variety of styles to high-light the unique potentialities of Jo, Meg, and Beth March as well.

The emancipation of the tomboy Jo's has been the most dramatic, and certainly no other type of daughter needed the new styles more, for a Jo in sheer nylon ruffles is a pathetic sight.

I remember one six-year-old who was nearly in tears when her mother led her into my office. She was ready to start first grade, and she was very unhappy about it. All summer long, and indeed for nearly five years, she had lived in blue jeans, and blue jeans she intended to wear come school or high water. Throughout a hectic morning of shopping, the daughter had sullenly maintained that her mother might buy as many dresses as she liked, but she would never get her to wear them.

Well, we cajoled her into coming back downstairs, and looking at the dresses her mother had selected, I began to suspect what was wrong. This was not an attractive child. She was tall and big-boned, with rather heavy features and pale blue eyes. Her only really lovely feature was a mop of hair the color of orange marmalade, which she wore in an untidy long bob, tucked behind her ears at the sides. It was not really the fact that she found jeans more comfortable than dresses which distressed her; with penetrating insight this little girl instinctively knew that the frills her mother loved made her look ridiculous.

Yet society takes a dim view of little scholars who turn up for the first day of school in dungarees and tee shirts. The fault was not really with the child, but with the impossible choice she was asked to make—looking like a second-rate girl or a poor imitation of a boy. What the tomboy needs above all else is the firm reassurance that she can be a woman without being a "little lady." (Mrs. Alcott, bless her, proved that when she created the very womanly Jo.)

In this case we began at the top. This Jo emerged from the beauty shop with the short, run-the-comb-through-it hair style that Jo's wear so well, if they have any curl to their locks at all. Had her hair been stick-straight, a short pony tail, perhaps with bangs, or the classic pigtails would have been a wiser choice.

Delighted with her "boy haircut," Jo became a very tractable little girl, and we headed for the sportswear department, where she was outfitted in well-cut chino pants and a white cotton turtle-neck shirt. It was boyish, certainly, yet paradoxically she began to look like a girl—and a well-turned-out one, too. As she turned round and round before the mirror she wore the loveliest, surprised, can-this-really-be-me? expression. This out-fit, we explained firmly, was for weekends and after school only.

For school we bought two dresses: a short-sleeved classic shirtwaist in rust jersey with brass buttons, and a long-sleeved version in broadcloth striped in rich fall shades of amber to brown. The effect, with that vivid hair, was breathtaking. It was important that both dresses were washable, strictly tai-lored, and supremely comfortable. Other types will put up with straps that slip, petticoats that scratch, or sleeves that bind, for vanity's sweet sake, but a Jo has no patience with clothes unless they are so comfortable that she can forget she is wearing them.

We also bought a flared suspender skirt of dark green cordu-roy and a matching twin sweater set. (The white turtle-neck shirt could be worn with this, and tailored broadcloth shirts could be added as the budget permitted.)

The transformation was simply unbelievable. It wasn't hard for an objective bystander to guess how often and how loudly Jo's mother had bemoaned her daughter's looks. Now our Jo smiled more easily, stood straighter, and every trace of sullenness and opposition drained away as she watched her mother's stunned surprise and delight.

More often than we care to admit appearance subtly in-fluences even a mother's feelings toward her child; grand-parents, teachers, and casual acquaintances are far more easily swayed. This is especially noticeable when there are two daughters, one far more attractive than the other, and many a case of real or imagined favoritism has had its roots in such obvious inequality. But if differences rather than resemblances are stressed, if each child is dressed as her own distinct and definite type, then comparisons are minimized and competi-tion almost eliminated.

The little girls huddled together in the Beth classification are particularly vulnerable to wounding comparisons.

A less sharply defined type than Jo, the Beth Marches are small for their ages, usually underweight, and often of very delicate skin coloring. "A sickly-looking child" a Beth may be labeled when overwhelmed with bulky fabrics and bold colors, but wisely selected clothes and hair styling will transform her from skinny to slender, from paleness to a Dresden delicacy.

Dainty and quaint are the keywords for Beth. Any hair style, any dress that may be described as charmingly old-fashioned—the dainty rosebud prints or tiny all-over Provincial patterns—are made to order for her. Emphasis should be on pastels or the new dark prints (particularly black-and-white) rather than on bold jewel tones or vivid plaids. But, surprisingly, touches of red sparingly used are wonderfuly flattering to pallid Beth.

Very full gathered skirts billowing out over starchy crinolines are perfect for her; high, collarless necklines, edged with lace or contrasting piping, are flattering; three-quarter sleeves or long sleeves are fine camouflage for thin little arms; and one of the most delightful touches for this little girl is an apron or a pinafore. And do be sure her dresses are short enough. If you sew, you will find that almost any style can be adapted to Beth, just by incorporating one or more of these features in the version you stitch up.

But whether you make or buy Beth's clothes, it's important that they fit, that they aren't too big, aren't too long.

Probably the nicest thing that ever happened to the Beths of this world is the home permanent. It is hard to believe, until you try it, how a thin little face takes on new sparkle, even new contours, when fine, straight hair is given fullness and soft waves. A long bob, not quite shoulder length, with a side part is flattering. So is a very, very long curly pony tail tied with a big bow, and perhaps softened by bangs. Or try two shorter pony tails or pigtails caught up in loops at each side of her head. But I've always thought the very loveliest way a Beth can wear her hair is the charming, old-fashioned style where the sides and front are brushed up and back and caught with a wide bow, the back falling long and softly curled.

One shiny spring morning I met a Beth I'll never forget—a four-year-old—on a most important day in her life. She had just that very morning left an orphanage to join her new family, and they had all—the new mother, new father, and social worker—come downtown to outfit her. She was a sweet and well-behaved little girl but certainly far from pretty, with straight black hair, tiny pipe-stem arms and legs, and a pale, pinched little face. But this mother knew her fashions, and she knew her little girl's type, too. When they left the store, that little Beth was wearing a very short, full dress of narrow black-and-white horizontal stripes with a perky little red suspender apron trimmed with narrow bands of the dress fabric. The skirt was buoyed up by crinolines, her hair was tied back with a narrow red velvet ribbon, her shoes were sparkling patent-leather Mary Janes, and she was as enchanting as a Kate Green-away portrait for the 1800's.

A Meg March, on the other hand, is as modern as Jon Whit-comb. Meg is also very, very grown up; usually she is a grave, dignified child, often large (or at least tall) for her age. Meg wears best the clothes that are styled like adult fashions—princess and empire waistlines, jumpers, duster-and-dress ensembles, dressmaker suits.

You will renounce, if she is to emphasize her very real charm, heavy napped fabrics, fussy ruffles and frills, wide sashes and puffy hair bows. Just as Beth must avoid the too-big look, Meg must be on guard (especially as she gets past the toddler phase) against the too-short babyish skirt, the strained-seam, overgrown, outgrown look.

If your daughter is overweight, never settle for less than the clothes especially designed and proportioned for chubbies; standard size-range dresses, however skillfully altered, never look quite right. A booklet entitled *Pounds and Personality*, by Dr. Gladys Andrews of New York University, offers excellent suggestions to the mothers who want to enhance their over-weight daughters, and is available without charge from a manufacturer who specializes in fashions for the chubby girl.

If you sew, you will find special patterns for chubby girls. In addition, many regular-size patterns give instructions for altering the width without destroying the proportions of the dress, and show more than one sleeve style or neckline or skirt. By applying the Little Woman Formula, you can combine details with a sure hand and make your handiwork a masterpiece of typecasting.

What about colors for modern-looking Meg? There is lots of leeway here, but very delicate pastels and very dainty prints just don't do anything for this big girl. Better lean toward rich, jewel-toned solids, grown-up looking floral prints or checks, and the vivid first-day-of-school plaids.

Meg, when she is very young, looks adorable in braids. As she grows up she usually coaxes to have her hair cut, and the grown-up styles—medium or short bob or page boy—suit her perfectly, especially if they rest on the foundation of curly hair or a good permanent. If Meg wears her hair long and straight, try a pony tail starting low at the nape of her neck. Or an Alice in Wonderland style held back by a clip or headband. Or cross her braids over her head in a coronet effect.

Have you noticed that nowhere have we suggested the short, straight Dutch-boy cut for any type? You have only to look in on any classroom to see that it's still a favorite fashion, but I have yet to see a child wearing her hair in this time-honored style who wasn't far more attractive when we switched to some other hair-do. Even more significant, I've never seen a truly beautiful child wearing a Dutch-boy cut, which raises the suspicion that it's a line of least resistance for mothers who have thrown up their hands in despair: "Janey is so plain, there really isn't much point in fussing!"

That's such a tragic mistake, for it's not the cuddly, adorable little dolls who need our "fussing." In fact, in real life, as in

Little Women, the little dolls—the Amy's—tend to be clothes conscious from a very early age, and far from encouraging their preoccupation with their mirrors, a soft-pedaling of emphasis on looks is all to the good.

As a matter of fact, Amy needs very little style advice. This bouncy, vivacious child (usually "just right" in height and weight and often blessed with either vivid dark coloring or pink-and-gold blondness) can wear any style, any color, most hair styles. She can change types so easily that one word of caution is in order: keep her dress, her hair, her accessories all from the same type classification. But some experimentation is good practice, for one of these days a sudden spurt of growth may change her type almost overnight.

Amy almost always has a passion for jewelry, perfume, and crimson nail polish—a passion her mother will do well to curb if she's to look like a pretty child instead of a caricature.

But the average or less-attractive-than-average child is never too young for *you* to be clothes conscious *for* her. Even at the layette stage, clothes make the woman. A beautiful baby—a pink-cheeked, cuddly Amy—may be cute as a kitten in just a diaper and hand-me-down shirt. But some of the infants who will grow into stunning and attractive women are simply not beautiful babies; the answer lies in dressing them to type even at this tender age.

Any baby who has only a fine fuzz where her crowning glory will someday flourish gives a tomboyish impression, and you can probably classify her automatically as a Jo. With as few frills as possible, with little tailored smock dresses or two-piece crawler sets, you'll achieve a charming effect, but don't go to the other extreme and choose outfits that prompt the is-it-a-boy-or-is-it-a-girl? query. Tailored bonnets are your ally until nature provides more bountiful curls, but be sure these aren't fussy.

There are infant Beths, too, and if delicate-looking baby Beth wears diminutive blue jeans and a little boldly-striped tee shirt, or a thick, fleecy pram suit, she will meet a constant stream of sympathy: "My, isn't she a frail little thing?" But dimity, voile, and batiste dresses in delicate pastels, worn with narrow-brimmed bonnets in sheer, airy fabrics, will change those comments to, "Isn't she just the daintiest little doll?"

I hope you've noticed that none of these transformations cost a cent; you must buy something for your daughter to wear, unless you live in a most unusual community, and the most becoming dress costs no more.

But there is one situation that may entail additional expense: you will soon find yourself so type conscious that hand-me-downs from big sister just won't look right to you. Unless, of course, your daughters are the same type, but alas, they seldom are!

Some dresses you can change astonishingly just by raising Beth's hem, or letting down Meg's, by ripping the sash off Jo's dress and substituting a leather belt. Such a little touch can make a world of difference. But some outfits you will want to discard ruthlessly.

We learned that lesson with our own Laurie, but in our case it was only a part of a far bigger problem, a problem faced by a great many mothers and daughters.

It was the most ironic moment for Laurie to dash through looking the way she did. Her father and I were making out a list of the clothes the girls would need for September. With Laurie starting kindergarten, it was quite a lengthy list. After all, you can't start a brand-new career dressed only in big sister's hand-me-downs, wearable though they may be. But looking at her as she streaked by, I wondered why we bothered.

As I raced her for the kitchen, I asked myself again, "Why can't she stay neat?" It was vital to get to the kitchen before she did. Laurie has a special—well, I suppose you might call it a knack—for disorganization. Where she moves, glasses shatter, chairs topple, stairs that stand immovable for everyone else rise up and strike her down.

In all justice, she does have a reasonable explanation. "I was in a hurry," she'll protest, to cover any situation. And she always is.

Laurie rushes, breathless, from adventure to adventure, certain that some wondrous mystery will escape her if she slows for a second. In a world where there are crickets to capture and clouds to chase and holes to peer into, delays for the humdrums of sleeping, eating, and dressing are merely tolerated. In fact, the eating and dressing (and I sometimes suspect the sleeping) are usually accomplished while jiggling impatiently from one foot to the other.

Now, we wouldn't change Laurie for the world. She glows. She generates love the way a puppy does. But it just isn't in her to care how she looks. We have never made a fetish of neatness in our family, but even with a baby sister and a tomboy big sister as bases of comparison, Laurie is in a class by herself.

That day I gave her a milk carton to put the caterpillar in, instead of the quart jar she was reaching for. I spoke sharply to her, too, I'm afraid. As we said earlier, a child's appearance does affect our attitude toward her, and I was finding it increasingly hard to be patient with Laurie, just because of the way she so often looked. At that moment her overall straps were hanging around her hips and her blouse was half unbuttoned. She had put her undershirt on wrong side out and backwards so a bright blue label waved gaily above her blouse collar, and her hair, as usual, covered most of her face.

"Push your hair back," I said, and realized too late that her hands were muddy!

Just to make everything perfect, when I went back to my husband and my lists he said, "Dear, can't you do something about Laurie? She always looks so coming-apart."

Before I could think of anything crushing to answer, he reminded me that I must have worked out knottier problems than this one when I was a fashion counselor, and there it was —the whole problem changed focus.

All this time I had looked on Laurie's lack of neatness as a character fault, and with great moral indignation had tried to weed it out. I think every parent has had that experience to some degree. We get so bound up emotionally with some irritating behavior trait that we fight our child instead of working on her side with practical, constructive aid. In short, in our family's terminology I had "gotten a thing" about Laurie's messiness.

But considered as a fashion problem, that messiness presented a challenge. Then and there I tore up the list of her fall-clothes requirements and got to work on several other lists. For the next two weeks I worked as hard at "styling" Laurie for neatness as I ever did at solving a customer's problems.

Her transformation was so swift and so gratifying that I herewith set it down for any mother who is beating her head against the same stone wall.

Hair. The first day of school Laurie marched off to class with braids. When I remember how I had thought she would go, with all that butter-colored hair caught up in a big bow (Laurie is a fragile Beth), I could have wept. Then I visualized how she would have looked coming home from school and I knew I was doing the right thing.

Socks. The new "stretch" anklets have eliminated the sagging cuff that used to testify to Laurie's strenuous tugging. And I bought them all exactly alike—plain white—so that even she can't mismatch them.

Underclothes. A little footwork unearthed several brands of undershirts with necklines cut low in the back as well as the front. Now no one can tell that four mornings out of five her shirt is still inside out and backward.

A source of confusion in the past had been that some of her panties had decorations in the front, others had ruffles in the back. Since she had outgrown them all, we started from scratch with all her little pants bearing their flowers, days of the week, and sundry ribbons in the front.

Shoes. That year we were stopped cold. Our doctor insisted she needed the support of oxfords for another year, which meant that her shoes were untied most of the time. Oh, she could tie a bow all right, but shoes just don't *stay* tied for Laurie. Ah, but once that year was past . . . straps!

Skirts and blouses. Straps and buttons were eliminated wherever possible. I found several attractive patterns and made jumpers with which she wears blouse slips (and what a heaven-sent invention *they* are!) and cotton knit pullover tops. In fact, the smartest outfit she has ("My teacher said I look nice, Mommy!") is a yellow corduroy jumper worn over a long-sleeved white sweater, with a yellow scarf tied loosely at her throat. And she still looks nice on the way home!

Dresses. When making her school dresses (and this would be equally applicable when buying dresses, of course) I find it helps to adhere to three rules:

1. Crease-resistant fabrics. Whether you're selecting ready-to-wear or yard goods, the new fabrics and finishes are just miraculous. *Our* mothers must find it hard to believe how fresh a school dress can look at the end of the day.

2. No buttons. The buttons are avoided by the simple expedient of substituting snap fasteners or zippers. One of the patterns I bought included the idea of a long zipper down the back, and I have carried it over into all other patterns ever since.

3. No sashes. Sashes don't stay tied, but the narrow patent-leather belts that so often come on ready-to-wear dresses do stay buckled. We strip such belts from old dresses before we give them to the Salvation Army or put them in the Goodwill bag, and find the old ones do nicely for all her new dresses each season.

Aprons. Each year I make her four colorful aprons in drip-dry fabrics. Actually they are wrap-around-and-tie jumpers, rather than aprons, with the neckline cut a little higher than the pattern directs, so that every inch of dress except the sleeves is covered.

Laurie's apron is laid out at night with the rest of her clothes, and she slips into it as soon as she is dressed in the morning, not taking it off until she brushes her teeth after breakfast. Aprons are priceless, too, for Sunday afternoons at Grandmother's house. One is slipped over her Sunday-school finery as soon as we get to Grandmother's. Since each is bright and colorful and carefully tailored, she looks cute as a button all afternoon, then whisks it off to emerge a glamour girl when it's time to go for a ride or to greet a Sunday-afternoon caller.

Hand-me-downs. As in most families with several girls, we keep a large carton in the attic filled with clothes that are waiting to be grown into. Here it was that we learned the difficult lesson I mentioned earlier. Laurie, tiny and slim, is the classic Beth. Naturally, most of the clothes that suit her husky older sister are all wrong for her. With a sadly limited clothes budget, it was a hard decision to make, but we decided that we would pass on only the outfits that were right for her. The difference was immediately noticeable in her play clothes. In toreador pants and more feminine tops, chosen to dramatize her, in clear light colors, she emerged looking as adorable as in her Sunday best. And we were careful to select tops that were meant to be worn with the tails out, since they would be.

It would be nice if I could say that her new wardrobe had such an effect on Laurie that she has changed her careless ways and has become neat and well groomed. But she hasn't, of course. She is still our breathless, rushing, clothes-unconscious Laurie.

But she *looks* like a different child. And looking different has made a difference—a difference in the way she feels, a difference in the way people feel about her.

Not that we want our daughters to think for one moment

that being beautiful is all there is to being a woman. There's tenderness and honesty and laughter and courage and compassion, too. But any little girl has a head start toward those other goals when she knows that she is, in the deepest sense, just as pretty as she can be!

CHAPTER 3

Beauty All Around Her, Beauty from Within

IN OUR TOWN there is a picturesque street called The Towpath. No, not a street, really, just a cinder road that ambles along parallel with the river, a dim tunnel through great oaks and elms and weeping willows, with the smell of the river heavy upon it. The houses lie on the bank like a row of lazy old dogs, their front paws on The Towpath, their shaggy behinds in the river. A few nearly naked children sometimes dig dispiritedly in the dusty yards, but for the most part The Towpath belongs to the old men—derelicts who wander up from Lower Barge Street to sleep in the deserted boathouses or under the rotting piers, or the old Canal men who ask only to sit out their days beside the water.

We were walking there, the two older girls and I, with

23

sketch pads and pencils, just because it is such a picturesque spot. As we walked, Lindy suddenly pointed across the road and breathed, "Oh, look; isn't it beautiful?"

Another row of houses squatted there, leaning against one another for support, as dilapidated as any we had passed, yet she was right. For at the far end one shack was different.

Its boards were weathered to an ancient gray like all the others, but it greeted the world with a freshly painted bright blue door, and the sagging window sills on either side were bright blue, too. On the window sills faded geraniums bloomed bravely in white pots. And from the doorway to the cinder road someone had marked out a careful path through the yard of hard-packed earth, then bordered it with white-painted smooth round stones.

I was so proud of Lindy that day, proud that she could see beauty in that brave, gay, pitiful little house on The Towpath, proud that she could see that wherever a single human being reaches for beauty or creates it with his own hands, there beauty is, no matter how imperfectly the attempt succeeds.

Isn't that something we all want for our children—a sensitivity to beauty, an awareness of beauty in the least likely places, a talent for beauty that "makes enchantment out of what's at hand"? It's not hard, really, once we decide what we're trying to achieve. The trouble is that each of us sees beauty so differently. How many faces it has, how many meanings!

For instance, we want to surround our daughters with beautiful things, but it is easy to fall into the trap of considering "beautiful" a synonym for "expensive." Whenever I see a woman who hounds her patient husband all his days, goading him on to make more money, so that their daughter can have "beautiful things," I'm tempted to tell her about Milly.

Milly and her daughter, Penny, lived in a rooming house the year I knew them, the year Penny was four. It was an ugly room, as most such rooms are: dark, cluttered, shabby, always a little grimy no matter how much Milly scrubbed. There was a bed, two dressers, a chair, the crib, the hot plate, and the washbasin. An ugly room.

But Milly wouldn't let that room defeat them.

Since life hadn't provided the lovely Penny with the world Milly thought her exquisite little girl deserved, Milly built Penny a world of her own: she built the dollhouse.

From the corner delicatessen she salvaged two sturdy wooden egg crates. When they were nailed side by side and topped with a peaked roof of cardboard, they formed four spacious rooms. Milly worked in a laundry, and evening found her tired, bone-tired, but every night, after their supper, Milly worked on the furniture. Out of spools and matchboxes and scraps of fabric she created it. Out of paper and cardboard and bits of ribbon.

She had got as far as making the dining-room table when I heard about it; sooner or later every tenant in the rooming house caught the enthusiasm of the project. The landlady offered paint cans that still held a little paint. When Second Floor Front's charm bracelet broke, she gave Milly the tiny silver telephone. When the store where I worked redecorated the executive suite, I salvaged the old green felt from the conference table for wall-to-wall carpeting. Another roomer clipped from magazines a dozen scenes of quiet gardens and rolling, well-kept lawns; pasted to the walls and framed by draperies, they became quite convincing windows.

Not that Milly accepted every offering! Colors must blend, proportions please the eye. Only fabrics of weight and elegance would do.

"A little girl has to know something besides this," she would say, encompassing with a wave of her hand the four stained walls and all they imprisoned. "I have to show her that some people live differently." In her way, in the only way open to her, Milly gave her child a beautiful, tasteful, private little world of her own. Caleb did the same thing for his little blind daughter, Bertha, in Charles Dickens' *The Cricket on the Hearth*, remember? Milly had only a sixth-grade education, but a deep inner wisdom whispered to her the same truth that Dickens knew and that modern-day social workers are rediscovering: it's not poverty itself that stunts a child's emotional growth, it's the ugliness that so often lurks in poverty's shadow that warps her.

In theory this should be as true for sons as for daughters, but in practice a girl is peculiarly at the mercy of her surroundings. Home is the center of her life to a much greater degree than it is for a son.

Even a very small boy, because of the more rough-and-tumble nature of his play, is likely to be happiest when he is out of the house, with space and freedom to spare. But watch a small girl at play; even in the yard she'll mark off a grassy corner to be her house and equip it with acorn cups, leaf plates, and mud pies.

As a boy grows, his interests widen, draw him more and more out of his home to the baseball diamond, the playground, the gym, or the weed-grown lot on the corner. But from the first afternoon she invites a little neighbor in for a cup of "tea," a daughter's social life revolves around her home. That's where she and her best friend come after school to giggle and whisper together. Later, home is where the gang gathers, where the sorority meets, where the marathon slumber party takes place. Even when she is away at Brownies or Camp Fire Girls or Girl Scouts, or church group meetings, much of her learning and activities will be centered around homemaking and child care.

Finally, when she reaches the age of dating, home is a place for dances. And then it will become a symbol of her own new womanliness when, as a poised young hostess, she can invite her date in at the end of an evening, confident of a welcoming atmosphere and pleasant, cheerful surroundings.

For sons, an attractive home is important, but for daughters, such a home is as vital as sun and air and water.

Fortunately lack of money is seldom the real obstacle to beauty in everyday life. More often it's an attitude that stops us.

"There's no point in fixing up the living room now," we say, "we'll wait to refurnish until the children can take better care of things." That might have been understandable twenty-five years ago; today it's unforgivable. Practical no longer means prosaic. Upholstered pieces are covered in bright scrubbable fabrics; rugs can be tossed into the washer; plastic table tops are cheaper than good wood and nearly indestructible. We now have Melamine dishes, plastic table mats, iron-strong curtains and bedspreads that drip-dry. Today a home furnished with children in mind can be a showplace, which is a boon to active little boys, of course, but a really priceless opportunity for little girls. The easiest way for a mother to develop a young woman's taste and discrimination is to have reared her in tasteful surroundings. We are the first generation of mothers who have found all the restrained and tasteful styling of quality furniture available in every price range. Even the unassembled, unpainted offerings are designed along the lines of fine furniture. Let's take advantage of all this.

In some homes we stumble over an even more negative attitude. These are the homes of men and women who profess to be above the mundane level of mere things. I knew a brilliant concert pianist who lived like that. She used no rugs on her floors, no curtains at her windows. The chairs and couches were piled with books, sheet music, and miscellany. To go from room to room meant blazing a trail through a maze of cardboard cartons and crates. "Above things" indeed! Adults should be intelligent and mature enough to be above such snobbishness. And that's all it is, just as truly as the opposite kind of snobbery, which makes a fetish of possessions.

The concert pianist I just mentioned was a mother of one of the most nervous, most unhappy children I have ever known. Coincidence? I think not. A child's surroundings affect her behavior in subtle ways. Several friends who have moved into half-completed homes in order to finish the interiors themselves have confided that in the torn-up atmosphere their usually well-mannered children turned wild and boisterous almost overnight. Our neighbors on the left had the same experience with their daughter's bedroom. When the unfinished attic where the girls had been sleeping progressed past the planning stage, when it finally boasted solid walls and a ceiling, an attractive floor, bright curtains, and bedspreads, the change in the girls was amazing.

For that reason alone I'm in favor of a slightly formal atmosphere in the living room if there's another, more casual gathering place available, too. There should be one place in the house—every parent deserves it and every daughter needs it— where the atmosphere commands our children to sit like ladies and talk quietly. Surely we can no longer say that we cannot afford to surround our daughters with beauty. Not when five dollars will bring a soft or sophisticated glow of color to the walls of one room with the new do-it-yourself paints. Not when packages of dye cost twenty-five cents at the drugstore or the supermarket and a ten-cent pack of flower seeds will yield a supply of fresh flowers for three or four months.

From such humble materials as orange crates, sanded and painted, we can create quite presentable bookcases and toy shelves for a child's room. (One of the smartest wall treatments I've ever seen consisted of shallow wooden grape crates painted in vivid primitive colors and nailed at irregular intervals all across an unused, blocked-off door, then filled with books, ivy, and the little owner's collection of china horses.)

No, we can't claim that it's lack of money holding us back.

If it's lack of imagination or courage, a large measure of each has been crammed between the covers of a book by Dorothy Draper. She calls it *Decorating Is Fun,* and by the time you get to chapter three you will have painted your front door and started rearranging the living room; I guarantee it.

Which brings us to the matter of skills. The woman who can braid rugs, refinish furniture, fit slip covers, and line draperies has a tremendous advantage, obviously, over one who can't. If you're just now learning that fact the hard way, you'll understand why part of Chapter 15 is devoted to steps you can take to equip your daughter with a fund of those skills which are like money in the bank when it comes to creating beauty in the home.

But of course beauty of *things* is not enough. We want more for our daughters than a beautiful shell around them. What else?

Well, manners, for one thing.

The trouble is that no other area of our lives has changed so radically in so short a space of years as have manners, so that too often we're not really sure what we should teach our children. I'm not talking now about the attitude behind good manners—that never really changes. I'm referring to the superficial aspect of manners, the questions of etiquette, of the "correct" thing to do. There the changes that have taken place in one generation are simply unbelievable.

Undoubtedly there are circles where little girls still curtsy, where little boys still bow. But not in most young American families, certainly.

What, then, for our daughters? Which of the rules we learned as little girls shall we pass on? Which are hopelessly outdated?

Obviously, I can't tell you. It depends on the part of the country in which you live, the social stratum in which you move, the schools your children attend, the way you yourself were brought up.

It depends, too, on how brave you are. It's a sad commentary on the state of American home life, but it's true. It takes courage today to take a stand on manners. If we go to one extreme, we'll be accused of snobbishness; if we go to the other extreme, we've failed our girls in a phase of their training that can make or wreck whole areas of their lives.

And not only of their own lives, for it is woman who sets the mood, determines the graciousness or gracelessness of a home. A man may take pride in being a rough diamond and still take equal pride in a home graced by a charming wife and beautifully brought-up children. But when the situation is reversed, when it is the woman who attaches no importance to the little niceties of life, then such a home may sadly limit her family's happiness and success.

These rules of the game that we call etiquette are superficial, of course, but in their very superficiality lies their importance to girls and women. During the course of a day or a year how many people do we come to know really well? Only a handful! Most of our contacts with other human beings *are* superficial. We have no way of knowing in these brief encounters whether the men and women we meet have hearts of gold; we can judge them only on the basis of their manners. And the burden—no, not the burden, rather the challenge—of most of these brief social encounters falls upon mothers and daughters . . . at parents' club meetings, on the church steps after Sunday-morning services, in the check-out line at the supermarket. Indeed, in these days of entertaining for business reasons, even the guests in our own homes are often strangers to us.

But when everyone plays the social game according to the same rules, the party, or the wedding, or any other social encounter will go smoothly. When even one rough diamond decides to throw out the rules, others are made uncomfortable and the happiest occasion may be marred.

I suppose that what I am really saying is this: *Being a lady never goes out of fashion.*

I believe that we owe our girls, first, a solid basic foundation of good everyday manners. There was a time when youngsters picked up this basic grounding unconsciously from the adults and other children around them. Today we live in such a fluid society that neighborhoods are no longer composed of families who live according to much the same set of rules. Our heterogeneous communities, as the sociologists designate them, are right and good. Eventually we'll no doubt work out a new code, acceptable to everyone. Meanwhile, though, it's hard on mothers.

The neighbor on your left tells your children to call her Marge. The neighbor on your right would be shocked by such familiarity.

Dinner at Susie's house calls for play clothes and is served in the kitchen. Dinner at Debbie's means a fresh, clean dress and candlelight. It's no wonder our children are sometimes unsure of their values—and of ours.

(Last night, one of Lindy's friends was watching her set the table and lay out the napkins. "Oh," she beamed, "you're going to have fried chicken!" When Lindy said, no, meat loaf, Sandy looked baffled and asked, "Then why are you having napkins?" Debbie was equally surprised, even shocked, about our napkins when she had dinner with us one night—because they were paper.)

What, then, are we to do?

I believe the answer is to stand at the highest level that is comfortable for us within our present community, to maintain the highest standard prevailing in the neighborhood. If we can manage to do that without teaching our daughters to be uncomfortable with families whose standards are different, our children will be at ease in the homes of all the children they know. And what if your standards are higher than the highest in the community? Then either your ideas of manners are unrealistic and snobbish or you are in the wrong community for you. (Or perhaps you don't know all your neighbors yet—frequently the nicest people are not the first you meet.)

But I feel we must go a step further. Good basic manners aren't enough. If we really want the best for these girls of ours, we will teach them the finer points of courtesy, the deeper rules of etiquette.

My husband and I don't choose to live stiffly, but it gives me a feeling of confidence to know that our girls are learning some of the amenities, no matter how busy and casual our lives.

Change for dinner? Heavens, I'm proud if I get their hair brushed and my apron off. But when there is a special occasion, we make it a very formal event, with party clothes and party manners. We take the girls occasionally to restaurants where the service is far more formal than it is at home. Our girls are never going to stare at a fingerbowl with a sinking heart, wondering how on earth they're supposed to use it. When we have a formal invitation to acknowledge, I seize that opportunity to teach them one more of life's little formalities that are so unimportant three hundred and sixty-four days of the year, but so terribly, agonizingly vital when we suddenly need to know. For such situations, every home needs a good standard etiquette book.

Often we hear the criticism that to have two standards of behavior, everyday manners and "company manners," is hypocritical. I think that's unrealistic. It seems to me that just as our daughters wear blue jeans for some occasions and velvet jumpers for others, so they need to be at home with both the everyday courtesies and the more formal points of etiquette.

Certainly we are trying to train our daughters in good, basic, everyday manners, to eat quietly and correctly, to make and acknowledge introductions graciously, to say "please," and "thank you," and "please excuse me," at the appropriate times. These things they are expected to *do*.

But there are other things we expect them to *know*, though they may have few occasions to practice them. Pouring tea, coping with receiving lines, the complicated protocol of weddings. Girls need to know, too, what is to be expected from boys in the way of good manners. The girl who expects proper manners from her dates commands respect.

Russell Lynes has said, "A lady is a woman who makes a man behave like a gentleman." But that is not a new idea. For generations the canny country folk of Ulster have observed that "manners are the beginning of morality."

But if there's a magic formula for endowing a child with these charming manners we're extolling, I've yet to find it. We depend on the combination of surroundings, example, and reminders.

Surroundings can be your strong ally, especially when you are stressing table manners. We have already touched upon the importance of beauty, and specific steps toward a dining room that inspires fine manners are outlined in Chapter 15.

Example, of course, is the backbone of any idea we want to put across to children. But being a good example isn't easy. When your head aches and the chocolate pudding has just boiled over and it's nearly four-thirty—when, in the midst of all that, your child brings a little friend home to play—it takes a real effort of will to greet them with the same gracious courtesy you would accord an adult. But the long-range results of that effort are so worth-while! Like the highly trained muscles that somehow fight on for a groggy boxer, without conscious direction, so years and years of training in good manners create a habit that requires little thought. That's how it can be for your daughter, if you start early and stick with it. For years and years is just how long it takes.

Reminding, let's face it, is just another word for nagging—years of tireless, ceaseless, cheerful, but relentless nagging. The cheerfulness is important, otherwise we defeat our efforts, so try to keep the reminders light and good-humored. We have a family trick that's reduced the irritations that too often go hand in hand with mealtime. When I see a flagrant violation of the rules I chant in exaggerated storytelling tones, "Once upon a time there were three little pigs." Each girl immediately checks herself—good training in itself—and the guilty party quickly makes the necessary correction. It saves tempers all around.

But eventually all those years pay off, they really do. Day after day it seems that everything we say falls on deaf ears and then—as suddenly as sunrise—we discover proudly that somewhere along the way our little Indian has become a little lady!

And ladies never go out of style. The little girl who enters first grade equipped with beautiful manners will win the affection of her teacher and her playmates long before they really get to know her. The teenager on the way to her first school dance needs a solid grounding in the "correct thing" if she's to sail into that crepe-paper-draped gym with relaxed confidence. The young bride finding her place in her husband's family will be either poised and dignified, or flustered and apologetic, depending to a large extent upon her ingrained manners. The young matron whose husband is rising steadily in his field often holds her husband's future in her hands when she pens a letter or plans a dinner party, or simply lunches with other company wives.

If we truly want the fullest, happiest life for our little girl now and when she is grown, we will give her an aura of beautiful manners to float around her wherever she goes.

Cultivated tastes, fortunately, have had a different fate from manners. They never seem to fall from popular favor.

Indeed, most parents approve so heartily of a "broad cultural background" for a daughter that they plan to buy her one when she graduates from high school—a situation roughly comparable to starting her on vitamins, orange juice, and milk that same year.

For culture, or a liberal arts education, or a cultivated taste, or what my economics professor used to call "a mastery of the useless arts," like good nutrition, is the result of years of absorbing the right nourishment. Start either process at eighteen and you've wasted the most important eighteen years.

Not that college, or a grand tour of Europe, or a course in music appreciation won't be valuable, too; but from the day your baby girl is born you can enroll her in a course of living that will find her, at high-school age, as cultured as many college graduates. We are truly educated, we often hear, when we know a little bit about everything and everything about something. Start early enough with your daughter and you can do better than that!

The key to this do-it-yourself education lies in borrowing a page from the school programs offered to gifted students in many states—courses often termed "enrichment." Instead of striving for a broad cultural background, education in depth becomes the goal. Not just a smattering of facts, but a deep understanding and appreciation of beauty as expressed through the fine arts of our own and other cultures.

It would seem a simple enough affair, this knowledge of beauty, when there are art galleries, museums, or at least mobile libraries, within reach of all but the most isolated homes, but sadly exposure is not enough. Director John Walker undertook a survey at the National Gallery of Art, in Washington, which shows that the average period of concentration by each visitor on each painting is *eight seconds!*

Is it any wonder we mutter, "I don't know anything about art but I know what I like?"

Let's just suppose, though, that you took the whole family to visit one room of a nearby art museum or art gallery. Once there, suppose that you all studied the paintings in that one room and decided on a single work that appealed to the whole family; that on your way out you stopped at the desk and bought a reproduction of that painting, even if only a postcard-sized reproduction; that during the next few weeks you dipped into the wealth at your public library to learn all you could discover about that painting. . . .

What else has that artist produced? What is the story of his life? What do art critics say about the painting? What did the artist's contemporaries have to say about his work and about this painting in particular? What was the political climate of his country during that period?

The whole family will become more and more fascinated the more deeply they delve, and by your next visit to the gallery to see "your" picture, you will all be well on your way to a liberal education!

No art gallery available? Subscribe to one of the monthly art "clubs" that offer perfectly exquisite reproductions accompanied by portfolios of information and interpretation.

Explore also, the probability that the art museum in your city is one of the many across the nation from whom original contemporary paintings and objets d'art may be rented on a monthly rotating basis.

Why settle for the standard plywood nursery cutouts when the walls of your child's room can glow with the rich beauty of Renoir's "Children in Rose and Blue," or Diego Rivera's "Children at Lunch," or Della Robbia's "Children Dancing"?

Or you may decide to subscribe to *Horizon,* that fabulous sister of *American Heritage.* It's fabulously expensive, too— $3.95 a copy, $18.00 a year, but a group of young families could split the cost. Or cheapest of all, and perhaps the most challenging, send for the catalogue of the Metropolitan Museum of Art or any of the top galleries. These culture-conscious institutions sell reproductions of an unbelievable variety of art works, sculpture as well as paintings, in a wide range of sizes and prices. Particularly worth having are their color transparencies, if you have a slide projector. The *American Art Directory,* available at your library, lists the addresses of such museums in your area.

In any case, this first adventure will lead you into so many fascinating byways that you'll be tempted to move on to another medium. And of course you should, but only after one man and his paintings and his world have become a part of you, and of your daughter, forever.

But art is not the only starting point. You'll have the same breathless sense of discovery in any field as one interest leads to another and another and another.

The natural temptation to begin with a project in which you yourself are something of an expert should be resisted. Your opinions will color your daughter's own judgment, and you will find yourself in a teacher-student relationship instead of that of two equally matched explorers. It might be well to wait until this new project is firmly established before you give your daughter the benefit of your superior knowledge.

Suppose you choose music as a starting point. First you will need a record player. Here again you might be able to halve the cost with a good friend who lives very near you.

Assuming you have the record player, before your baby is born is not a bit too soon to collect her musical layette. You might begin with lullabies. If your baby showers didn't net you that exquisite album of lullabies, "Golden Slumbers," do treat yourself to it. The art work, the introduction which tells the story of each lullaby, the music itself, all are perfectly beautiful and perfectly executed. Another you'll like is "Lullabies from 'Round the World," which, if your baby has an older brother or sister, can lead into reading about one of the countries represented, hearing other folk music that is sung there, even, perhaps, learning a few words and phrases in the language. (There are records for that, too! Especially fine is "French for Children.")

Not that you'll limit your baby to children's records. If you have no reason to trust your own judgment in musical matters, go or write to the record-lending department of the nearest large public library. The sound-steeped young ladies there will be delighted to map your course, selecting the classical music that's soft and simple and uncomplicated and soothing to small new ears. Three that our three children loved when they were babies are: "Eine Kleine Nachtmusik" by Mozart, "Rosamunde Overture" by Schubert, "Hungarian Dances" by Brahms, and, of course, his eternally right "Lullaby."

Not for a moment do I maintain that we want for our daughters an exclusively classical musical education. For most of us a balanced diet is the ideal in this as in other realms. The trouble is that in terms of hours of exposure to music the cards are stacked against "good" music. All their lives our daughters will be exposed to more trash than pleasant music, and to more pleasant music than great music. In order to maintain some semblance of balance, we parents must weight the scale in favor of classical music.

But again exposure is not enough. That same cooperative librarian can supply you with colorful stories of the lives of the great composers, with pictures, and with reference books that will offer rich soil for the sort of deep digging we described in connection with art.

A child who hears the best in music all around her, all her life, who is familiar with the men and the times and the cultures that produced this music—such a child won't need to be told to "appreciate" good music. She will have a storehouse of beautiful sound within her, as much a part of herself as her bones and her blood.

When it came to books, the earliest settlers of this land had few from which to choose, yet we produced some magnificent men with magnificent minds nourished almost wholly on the Holy Bible and the Bay Psalm Book. But how they knew those few books they had! Even the children committed to memory more of the Bible than most adults are even familiar with today. Oh, I know all the arguments against learning by rote; that's not what I propose at all, though I knew a man in Kansas City once, a gaunt man with the pall of a Japanese prison camp still upon him, who insisted that that now-discredited custom of reciting from memory saved his life. Of 270 men, only a handful fought to survive, and won. Only a handful retained the drive, the life spark that kept them alive through two years they couldn't possibly live through, and he credits the indestructible words of wisdom and beauty which the men carried in their memories as the force that sustained them.

"We spent hours just reciting," Frank would tell you. "One guy would say a poem, or a piece from the Bible, and then the rest of us would learn it, too. You'd be surprised how far back you can remember when there's nothing else you dare to think about. 'Who has seen the wind . . .' stuff like that from fifth, sixth grade. But there were a couple of fellows there, real educated, used to say whole pages out of Plato and Epictetus. Another guy was crazy about Thoreau.

"That Shakespeare!" Frank always added wonderingly. "His plays never made much sense to me when I read them in school, but you think about something like Hamlet's soliloquy in a hole like we were in, where dying sounds pretty good, and —well, he has something to say, believe me."

Of course the great classics have something to say to us; they have spoken to men's hearts for generations, for centuries. That's why they are classics. And one of the finest gifts a parent could give a teenager, I truly believe, would be a membership in, and textbooks for, the Great Books Course in her community.

But an even greater service would be to give her fifteen or sixteen years of the classics *before* she's a teenager. Children's classics, at first. There are some fine sets available, but if you build a library of individual books *you* loved as a little girl, your love of them will gild them in your daughter's eyes.

It saddens me to see these old favorites put on phonograph records, even when they are superbly narrated. That close hour when a mother reads to her little girl offers one of the most precious and heartwarming relationships we can know. And do buy some *beautiful* books. There are so many attractive twenty-five-cent books and dollar editions available of new, modern books, and every child should have them; but a little girl needs a few books that are quite special—books that must be handled with clean hands while sitting in the big chair. Books meant to last a lifetime, bound with leather's richness, illustrated with delicate pastel tracery or bold pen strokes, pictures that will rise to meet her from the past some night when *her* little girl clambers into her lap and begs, "Mommy, tell me a story." Every year the Children's Services Division of the American Library Association selects the most beautifully illustrated book for children, to be awarded the Caldecott Medal. Your librarian has a list of all the past medal winners she will be glad to give you, and you will find that every one is a perfect tresure.

But of course you can't judge a book by its illustrations; in the final analysis the worth of any book is measured by how well it meets the needs of your child.

A book you read and reread as a child may strike no spark in your daughter beyond the interest it arouses in the unfamiliar concept of her mother as a little girl. On the other hand, a book you choose quite at random may be one that will go straight to her heart and offer comfort or inspiration just when she needs it most.

I've already spoken of the amount of nagging our Laurie underwent because of her affinity for mud. One day we came across a little story by Margaret Wise Brown called "The Good Little, Bad Little, Clean Little, Dirty Little Pig," a story that so met Laurie's need for assurance that she could be loved though messy that she asked for it night after night after night. Nearly every child has had a similarly moving experience. Surely this is one of the benefits Strickland Gillilan had in mind when he wrote, "Richer than I you can never be; I had a mother who read to me."

More than any other generation, we have at our fingertips so many aids to start us off in the right direction toward en-

dowing our daughters with a lifetime love of books. One of
the most easily accessible of these guides is the up-to-date list,
maintained by every library, of new and appealing books for
children.

It seems to me that no discussion about books would be
complete without mentioning *Highlights*. This delightful
monthly, more book than magazine, has been circulating for
fourteen years, but it is a recent discovery in our home and we
are all tremendously impressed with it. Not only is it a children's magazine of exceptionally high quality, but it whets the
girls' interest in so many subjects, which sends them, of course,
to the local library or their home bookshelves.

You also may find valuable ideas in the excellent and comprehensive book about books, *A Parent's Guide to Children's
Reading* by Nancy Larrick. It includes sections on reading
aloud, how to select a reference book, how reading is taught in
the schools today, where to obtain magazines, pamphlets, and
films that will instruct and entertain both parents and children, and how to develop a home library.

But no matter how complete your child's home library may
be, it's never too early to start her in the public-library habit.
Even a toddler is ready to learn about libraries. At first only the
hushed quiet will intrigue her, but soon she'll notice the decorations on the bulletin boards, the vivid posters. If you select
one read-aloud book for her each time, and plan a story hour
with it when you get home, she will learn to look forward to
those trips with real excitement. (Library books should never
be "read" by tiny tots—it's unfair to put such fascinating, rus-
tling temptation right into their eager little fists.)

At four or five she'll be ready for the story hour at the library,
in the care of an older child, or while you read nearby.

There's a perfectly delightful little book called *Rosa Too
Little* by Sue Felt that will appeal to your child when she is
ready for her own library card (first grade in most systems).

Rosa will lead your child into this exciting new world on a very personal level.

The summer after your child leaves first grade she should be ready for the Summer Vacation Book Club at the library, and there's another new world to explore!

One delightful aspect of all this diligent planning is that you only have to do it once; as each new child arrives, the book-loving older children take over her library education themselves.

Most schools offer some instruction in the techniques of library use—the mysteries of card catalogues, Readers' Guide—but like most such instruction on a mass level, it doesn't start early enough for many girls. So when your young lady has learned to read and is anxious to branch out on her own, ask your librarian for a good pamphlet or book on library usage and explore the library with your child. All the accumulated knowledge of the ages is reposing there, and you have only to help your child forge a key.

But we mustn't make the mistake of providing only children's books for children. How much we would miss on Christmas Eve, for instance, without Marley rattling his timeless chains, without the majestic language of the Nativity according to Luke. So much reading that she doesn't fully understand touches a child's emotions deeply, or delights her sense of rhythm or rhyme. Or a child who has already met Ludwig Bemelmans' intriguing little Parisian, Madeline, might enjoy his *My Life in Art*, though there would be much that she could not understand. Carl Sandburg, Betty MacDonald, Rudyard Kipling, and countless other writers have produced works for both children and adults, and for many precocious juvenile readers one will lead to the other.

With books as with music, you will find it wise to tip the scale in favor of "good books." The pleasant books that while away an aimless hour are always at hand; your child will find these without your help. But in promoting the reading of really worth-while books, the same education-in-depth concept we described in connection with art and music will make her reading more meaningful. If a classic is just a title on a required reading list, to be skimmed and reviewed in as little time and with as little thought as possible, a change in *your* attitude may make all the difference. Try turning that book into a family research project, as you did with art. What can you find out about the author, about his background, his attitudes, his personal life? What have the critics said about him and his works? Why has this book lived through the years? By this time the whole family will be so intrigued by the subject that they may want to take turns reading aloud after dinner, or, at the very least, hearing the book report before it's turned in to the teacher. Of this you can be sure: it will be a thoughtful, perceptive book report, and the classic itself will have added its wealth to your daughter's cultural background.

Before we leave the subject of books let's take a long look at this business of memorization. I'm well aware that there are two schools of thought on the value of learning by rote. However, we are in the midst of a project here at our house which has filled me with enthusiasm for the committing to memory of beautiful passages of poetry and prose in the old-fashioned manner. It began when Joyce, our youngest, who "goes to school" on television's Romper Room School, eagerly brought forth each evening at the dinner table the little rhymes and songs she had learned that morning. Almost without knowing how it happened we found ourselves encouraging the older girls to memorize a few lines every day. At first they were responsible for four lines, then six, at the present time they are proudly presenting eight lines, and both of the older girls have noticed that this training in mental discipline and alertness is reflected in their work at school.

At first we chose at random from books lying about the house. Every home contains a wealth of material suitable for this type of memorization. But just two weeks ago I came across a book in our public library that was so perfect for the program on which we have embarked that we are now selecting all the material from the covers of *A Treasury of Golden Memories*. Edited by Kenneth Seeman Giniger, it is truly what the name promises—a treasury of all those "pieces" which our grandfathers and grandmothers learned and which we remember from our own school days. Our girls are aware only that this is a challenging new family project, but we believe that the training it provides and the familiarity with beautiful language and great minds which they are experiencing will be of lasting value for all the years of their lives.

"The best things in life are free," we quote, yet often we let the libraries, museums, and art galleries of our town lie idle while we scrimp and pinch to pay the premiums on an education policy, or to make deposits in a trust fund for our child's education.

"What we will be we are now becoming," we quote, yet we miss this chance to fill our daughters so full of good art, good music, good books that there is no room left for trash.

There's nothing wrong with the proverbs we mouth, if only we will give them more than lip service. Comic books, and C movies, Mickey Spillane, and rock 'n' roll—none of these need discourage us if we start early enough to teach our children to love beauty, to understand it, to search for it, to create it. In fact, we might well add one more truth to the others, not only quoting it, but acting upon it:

"Train a child in the way he should go; and when he is old he will not depart from it."

The trouble with a broad cultural background is that it occasionally turns a girl into a broad cultural snob. Her neighbor, who prefers musical comedy to opera, Agatha Christie to Dostoevsky, Grandma Moses to Monet, is treated to her scorn, though she may be twice the woman our smug little critic is.

The danger implicit in a training in beautiful manners is

much the same. Ritual may become more important than feeling, and a hollow, empty set of beautiful manners become a substitute for a beautiful soul.

The result, and the result we must avoid at all costs if we want happiness for this young life we cherish, is a girl whose ideals of beauty have no connection with the real world. Unless she can marry an independent income and be surrounded by old masters, first editions, and full-time-gardener landscaping, she will always feel that life has cheated her. The beauty that lies in simple, ordinary everyday living she cannot comprehend.

There's one in almost every neighborhood, and I am sick to death of such women's pity and contempt. They hate housework because the ugly drudgery of it offends their sensitive, artistic souls; those of us who gladly give our lives to homemaking must therefore be dull, insensitive clods.

I've learned there's no use arguing with these exalted few. Something was lacking in their early training, that's all, and there's little we can do to show them what they're missing. But we can see that we don't impose such narrow standards of beauty on our own daughters that they turn out the same way.

We must help them see the less obvious beauty around them—the strong, clean tiredness of their muscles after a really hard job done well, rain on the attic shingles, the polished grain of walnut.

Too often we're ashamed of sentiment, most of all in our own job of homemaking. But fortunately very little girls haven't had time to distinguish between exalted beauty and common beauty. If we indoctrinate them young enough, they'll never learn that particular brand of snobbery.

One spring day, one of those soft blue April days that are so beautiful they hurt, I was washing the winter grime from the kitchen windows when the girls came home from school. Laurie stood in the driveway, leaning 'way back (we live on the second floor) so she could see me sitting there on the sill high above her.

"Whatcha doing?" she called, the way children will when they know but want to hear your voice.

"I'm letting in the sunshine," I called back. Where the phrase came from at that moment I don't know. But I know how it made both of us feel. It showed in Laurie's smile and I felt it in my voice. I was letting in the sunshine. *I was doing something important and beautiful.*

Since that April day I've had great respect for the wonderful and terrible power of words. I try to put them to work, the words, to lighten our work and brighten the hours of each day. "Polishing up this living room before Daddy gets home" gets toys off the floor more cheerfully than "cleaning up" ever did, and we don't dust any more, we shine the tables.

We can collect phrases just as we collect recipes. We can make a conscious effort to think of our work in romantic terms. And when we do, our work will take on glamour in our own eyes and stature in the eyes of our family and the world. This attitude will encourage our daughters to cultivate beauty wherever it is found in their rounds of daily living.

Kahlil Gibran has said in *The Prophet* that "Labor is love made visible." Certainly nowhere is that more true than in the labor of making a home for the ones we love best.

Beauty of service, we might call it. It's a value many of us need to relearn. We need not give our lives dramatically and wholly to a cause, like Dr. Schweitzer or Florence Nightingale, or a missionary in some far land. As mothers we give a little of ourselves each day. Have you heard the story about a visitor who watched in revulsion while a nun in Viet Nam dressed a leper's sores?

"I wouldn't do that for a million dollars," he gasped.

"Neither would I," she answered.

Any mother mopping up the floor beside a sick child's bed, or rinsing out a badly soiled diaper, knows what she meant.

Some of the things our job of mother requires of us are ugly, but that makes our calling no less beautiful.

"Labor is love made visible." If we can teach a daughter to see beauty in the work she does at home now, and in all the creative areas of developing a home and family that will be at least a part of her career in the years to come, then we will have surrounded her with beauty that will last her all her life.

CHAPTER **4**

No Chores at Our House

W<small>HEN</small> the doorbell rang that day I was up on the ladder washing the kitchen walls, so I just called out, "Come in!" My husband warns that we'll all be murdered in our beds (or on our ladders) if I persist in doing that, but it saves a lot of steps. Besides, it's always someone like this very sweet gray-haired woman, equipped with sensible shoes and brief case, making a radio-listening survey.

After she had asked all her questions, and as she was leaving, she turned back to the kitchen and said wistfully, "This certainly makes a pleasant picture." I gathered that she meant the three little girls and me, all splashing around getting the kitchen clean.

"I just don't know," she sighed. "I never could get mine to

cooperate." Well, I'm not sure ours *cooperate* either, but they certainly do love to *work*.

Our method is a simple one which could be adopted by any determined family: the secret is to be inconsistent, inefficient, and enthusiastic.

Oh, we tried that business of assigned chores. We even kept charts with neat little squares for the days of the week and shiny gold stars to paste in the neat little squares. But our girls never won any stars. They loved their charts. They always dragged visitors to the kitchen to see them (Joyce and Laurie had a picture cut from a magazine showing each job, since they couldn't read, and their charts were really works of art!) The trouble was, I still did all the work around the house—and nobody gave me any gold stars, either.

But that was two years ago. Now, instead of Doing Chores, our girls Keep House—and what a difference!

My first venture into the exploitation of child labor came when Joyce was two and Grandmother gave her a new toothbrush, pink, with a little bunny on the handle. One morning while I mopped the bathroom floor, Joyce dipped her new toothbrush in my scrub pail and began industriously scouring the baseboard. Now it just so happens that I do some of my best daydreaming while I mop, so it was quite a while before I noticed all this activity; when I did, there was a corner and several inches of baseboard just as white as it could be. I would have sworn that our dingy old paint could never look like that again. Heaven knows it hadn't for a long time.

Well, the next day we bought Joyce a new toothbrush (pink, with a duck on the handle), and every time I mop the bathroom or kitchen floors she does the baseboards with the bunny one. Not around the whole room, of course. She loses interest after about a foot and a half. But by staggering the place where she began each time, within a few weeks the baseboards of those two rooms were absolutely spotless. She even dug out those little black corners in the molding of the kitchen cupboard doors, and the sneaky little spaces behind the pipes and along the front of the stove.

Don't ever sell that Tom Sawyer business short—it wasn't any time at all until Laurie and Lindy were down on their hands and knees, too (but I supplied *them* with *old* toothbrushes). The beauty of it is that even three of them can't spill much water with a toothbrush. But of course they can splatter a lot. Temperature permitting, underpants and old socks are basic garb for the girls. We tried bare feet, but they skid out from under on wet linoleum.

Because of the splatter hazard, I always arranged to mop the floors while they cleaned woodwork. It was just more convenient that way—I hadn't yet discovered that working together was the key to the success of the whole scheme. When I saw how much these little helpers could accomplish (they were two, five, and six then), I expanded operations.

Polishing the silver, for instance, proved to be almost as much fun as making mud pies in the garden, and a lot more grown up. But I soon learned to suggest that we shine up only the serving dish, or polish only the teaspoons. Not that we have so much silver; but little girls take best to domesticity in small doses.

Not only our girls, but all the children on the block wanted to get in on the floor waxing. I spread the paste wax, let it dry, then turned all comers loose with pairs of Dad's worn-out wool socks over their shoes. Many other activities that seem to be play can really be of help to a busy mother. For instance, feather pillows emerge plump and fluffy after a rousing pillow fight!

Many household jobs that at first glance would seem to be routine are really rich opportunities for training a daughter in the more subtle skills of womanship. Laying out her clothes for the next day, each night at bedtime, is an example. On the surface, a dull job, certainly; but look deeper and we find a whole course in color and harmony, in good grooming, in good taste. There is probably no other area of our children's lives in which the rate of growth differs so markedly as in the ability— and willingness—of our daughters to dress themselves. Many a little girl takes complete responsibility for dressing herself by the time she is three while her sister may still need a great deal of help even at the age of five. But once she starts school every little girl should be made to realize that her clothes and her grooming are now largely her own responsibility. No matter how carefully we select our daughter's wardrobe, our efforts are in vain unless each morning she starts off with an appropriate dress appropriately accessorized, and the foundation for this well-put-together look is laid the night before.

It may be that you will still decide the dress that you wish her to wear. In that case her responsibility may consist of selecting a handkerchief, socks, and barrettes that blend well. This is a particularly happy arrangement if your daughter is a meticulous, careful child. If she is a bit on the slapdash side, it may work out better for you both if she selects the dress she would like to wear and leaves to your more orderly mind the assembling of the accessories which will do most for her dress. All this takes only a few moments the night before, though it seems to take twice as long when left for morning, and you will find that in establishing this simple routine which leaves plenty of time tomorrow for a leisurely breakfast and a calm start for the day you are developing patterns of lifetime value.

These same lifetime patterns are, of course, the real guiding motive behind any mother's desire to have her daughter help with all phases of housework. Nearly all of us have seen the difference between a bride who enters her new life with a good basic grounding in household skills and one who is totally ignorant of the job ahead. I was convinced that in welcoming my girls into my workday I was rendering them a real service. But, unfortunately, like the head of many an expanding business, I got too ambitious.

"Why don't you wash that window sill in the hall?" I

would suggest when one of them came whining that "it's rain-ing and there's nothing to do and all those toys in my room are dopey." It didn't work. I finally came to understand that children want to work with us, not for us; that when it's a joint project, when the rallying cry is "Let's all pitch in and tackle this bedroom," then they love it.

And what a difference it has made in our house, admittedly not the most spotless on the block these last few years! You know how it is when the children are babies—you have to de-velop a few blind spots. Even cutting corners to a perfect cir-cle, there's never enough time during those years.

I read somewhere that those post-partum blues are caused by a chemical imbalance of the ductless glands. Don't you be-lieve it! They're the result of dishes soaking in the sink, diapers soaking in the tub, fuzz balls collecting under the dresser, and never enough money, never enough sleep, never enough time.

But when things can't possibly get any worse they always start improving, and suddenly there we are: our older offspring are in school at least half the day, the youngest is out of diapers and reasonably reasonable about such activities as overturning lamps and upsetting ash trays. But do we relax and enjoy it? No!

A surprising reaction sets in. After years of just trying to catch up, a new goal shimmers on the horizon: a shining clean, really clean-in-the-corners-clean house. Now that we have caught up with our work, we long to get ahead of it. And that's where having daughters pays dividends again.

So often all we need is a *little* help. Just one job out of the way can change our whole attitude from swamped to serene. Now we could get sons to handle that extra job, but when we are working side by side with our little girls, we can bask in the satisfying thought that they will bless us for this painless form of on-the-job training all their lives. (Someday an envious neighbor will ask one of your daughters, "How on earth do you handle it all so smoothly, and you a brand-new bride?" And then won't you feel smug?)

"But," mothers keep telling me, "it's quicker to do it myself." That's not so. Not if you choose the right areas for initiation. Of course, if you're going to start your five-year-old out on baking a batch of gingerbread . . .

However, take washday. Someday try stretching a low rope above a grassy corner of the yard (less mud if something drops) and let your toddler hang all the socks, take them down when they're dry, and sort them by pairs. We often do that, and I figure it saves me at least twenty minutes, though it keeps little Joyce contentedly busy for an hour. We both are rewarded with that warm feeling of closeness mothers and daughters know in such moments, too, which is quite as nice as the time saved.

Or take vacuuming. Children love to use the crevice tool on radiators and baseboards. They do a fine job on upholstered pieces (including the box springs and mattress that the manufacturer said should be cleaned monthly, remember?). They can even get the rugs well begun for you.

"Thank you, Susie," you can say. "You've gotten all the worst of it up; I'll just put on the finishing touches." And there you are with your rug-cleaning time cut in half. (If the vacuum is a tank type, one section of the wand removed will cut it down to size.)

And how long has it been since the bookcases were thoroughly cleaned? For a wonderful rainy-day project, have your youngsters pile all the books on the floor, then while you wash the shelves the children can vacuum or dust the books, turns at the vacuum being strictly rationed. When the shelves are dry, little children will love to arrange the books back in place according to size or color; older helpers will want to work out elaborate classification systems by subject or author's name. In either case you will find the big job finished while you have gone on to other tasks, resulting in a real timesaving, even allowing for all the time you and the children will spend on the floor leafing through neglected old favorites. That's the sort of day that builds memories for later years, memories that will shape your children's children's lives.

At our house one of the best-loved holidays of the year is Thanksgiving, when the girls do easily more than half of the actual work, and feel terribly adult and important. Little Joyce rubs salt and butter onto and into the turkey, puts the napkins at each place, polishes fruit for the centerpiece, has even graduated to stuffing celery with softened cheese spread. The older two stuff the turkey, truss it (no harder than lacing shoes, after all), whip hard sauce for the plum pudding, set the table (resplendent with elaborate place cards they've been laboring over for days), and handle a hundred other grown-up tasks. You can imagine how much more fun the day is for me, how much more time I have to spend in the living room instead of the kitchen, and how much more Thanksgiving means to all of us.

But this is just a small part of what we hope to gain. Our children will learn to work, for one thing. Employers all across the country are complaining that young women today just don't know the meaning of a day's work for a day's pay. And small wonder. In our big-city, small-home lives we often have only manufactured chores to take the place of the old-time family partnership. But children don't want busy work. They want to *help,* to know that they are needed, that the work they are doing would go undone or fall on overburdened shoulders if they were not around to do it. And they need to know it now, not someday in the future when we are convinced they can do a job as well as we can.

All our shiny new appliances make that so hard, for most of them are too intricate or too dangerous or too costly for tiny hands to manipulate. Well, here's how we try to minimize that problem.

Each child starts at the most primitive level of each task,

progressing to gadgets, then to electrical appliances as she matures.

When it comes to making frosting, small Joyce mixes and kneads with her fingers and a spoon, Laurie with an egg beater, and Lindy with the electric mixer (under hovering supervision!). The same progression applies to washing clothes: Joyce washes out doll clothes in a little basin; Laurie does the wool socks and hand washables with a scrubbing board or the sock stretchers, as needed, constituting her equipment; Lindy can handle each phase of the entire wash, though she isn't allowed to use the wringer unless I'm right beside her. I hope that someday we'll have an automatic washer, and when we do they'll all learn to use it, and a mixer and a blender, and all the other magic devices. But meanwhile they are learning a lesson we too often neglect in this land of plenty; it's vital that our children learn that work can be done without appliances. That rugs can be broom-swept and clothes rubbed clean. That seams can be stitched by footpower or fingerpower. That all biscuits don't come in little twist-open cartons.

Of course we all dream that when our daughters marry they will move into fully-equipped dream houses, staffed with mechanical servants and a cleaning woman on Thursdays. Although the houses have changed, that dream has been the same for generations of mothers. Somehow we never visualize them in Quonset huts or trailers on some far-away campus or Army camp, as so often happens. Let's be realists. Let's show them several ways to do each job, at various levels of equipment. Perhaps then we'll have fewer disillusioned brides, weeping frustrated tears over balky, obsolete equipment for which they've had not the slightest training.

We even recruit our neighbors and relatives for this "training program," when they have some apparatus we don't have. And that gives our daughters another plus. I not only hope that they will learn to work, but that they will learn to work with another person and for another person. And I hope that they will learn that there is more than one right way to do any job. They may even learn a better way, though I'd hate to admit it, than they learned at home. Ordinarily I rule the housekeeping side of our lives with an iron hand; someone has to be the Chief Executive, so we do things my way. But I'm fairly easy to convince if one of them brings me a better way—and they do, surprisingly often.

In fact, Lindy's resourcefulness cost her a lucrative five-cents-per-week job. We have one of those monstrous clawfoot bathtubs, the kind you simply cannot reach all the way under and behind no matter what contortions you attempt. So we bought a long-handled brush and Lindy was paid five cents to crawl around on her stomach and retrieve the lint, dropped washcloths, and miscellany that collect there. One day she tried the crevice tool of the vacuum and found it worked perfectly. In the manner of big industries, where workers are rewarded for efficiency suggestions, Lindy received a lump-sum settlement of $1.00 and now no one minds doing the job "for free."

Incidentally, that loathsome task was the only one for which we've ever paid. In theory, the girls don't have to help. I prefer to maintain the fiction that working together is a privilege which they'll forfeit if they refuse too often. But like all organizations that rely on the work of volunteers, we have had our problems. Some of our mutinies had been put down with dispatch. Once Laurie looked at me out of the corner of her eye and said, with elaborate casualness, "You know, I've been thinking I don't have to set this table. I mean, no one *makes* me do it."

Just as casually I answered, "I know. That's a good feeling, isn't it? This afternoon when I started to bake the banana cake I thought the same thing, 'I don't have to do this.' But then I thought about how much pleasure it would give all of us, so I did."

Lindy's rebellion centered around going to the store. For several weeks she manufactured an excuse every time I needed her. When she finally realized that I had simply stopped asking, she was informed (and I'll admit it was a gamble) that she could run no more errands for a full week.

That incident got me started thinking about changing around to suit the job to the girl. Laurie loves to go to the store; every trip offers potential adventure. Lindy, we began to realize, clearly does not enjoy errand running. When we discussed familiarity with the arts, we mentioned the desirability of knowing a little bit about everything and everything about something. I began to wonder whether the same principle applied to training in the useful arts might not make the difference between competent, efficient houseworkers and creative homemakers. True, efficient housework is the skeleton of homemaking, but it takes a special brand of magic to clothe the bare bones of it with the flesh of *caring*. Magic though it is, it's not new magic. It is just the pride, the sense of personal identity, of knowing we do one thing superlatively well.

Today's girls can do more things well then Grandmother ever dreamed of, much less attempted, and these skills have resulted in a generation of wonderfully versatile homemakers. But too often our daughters grow up feeling that making a home is a science. It's not. It's an art.

If we start very early, guided by our daughters' preferences for one job over another, we can help each child to become an expert in one field of homemaking; in short, we can help her to develop a specialty.

Here is your chance to set your daughter on the path to future contentment with her role, if that role turns out to be homemaking. So many young wives complain of frustration, discouragement, boredom, that you would think that they held the most menial jobs. Yet others, in the same set of circumstances, glow with quiet enthusiasm and love the lives they lead. It would be ridiculous oversimplification to say that a bride's attitude toward housework was the root of the problem, nevertheless, in many, many marriages, that attitude will be a disrupting factor.

In the early developmental years of the employee-relations field one of the first discoveries the personnel men made was that absenteeism, high turnover, and low morale all could be corrected by instilling pride in the job, and that basic to pride in the job was skill in the job.

You will find that the skill need not be spectacular to be gratifying. My twelve-year-old niece has an impressive knack with that most prosaic of implements, the iron. While the rest of us shop cannily for drip-dry and no-iron fabrics for our youngsters' clothes, all four of Martha's sisters march off to school in starched ruffles, or in the case of her brother, in an immaculate white shirt and sporting a crease in his freshly laundered jeans. Martha's mother started her off when she was five, with a warm iron and all the family handkerchiefs. Now she does nearly all the ironing for her big, noisy, well-kept family.

Martha's mother hates to iron. Surprisingly, this is often the earth in which a child's special interest flourishes, perhaps because we are more willing to let them try their very young hands at a job we'd like to duck, or perhaps because here they need not compete with Mother's specialty.

It is a rare experience in the childhood of any girl to discover that there is anything that she can do better than the adults around her. It is a stimulating experience, too, and one which we must not be too proud to allow her.

"Here is something I can do really well!" That's a proud and happy statement, isn't it? It may be that your daughter packs her own lunch and brings the most imaginative, unpredictable, tradable lunch. Or she may have a thumb so green that her little doorstep garden and your window shelves have become a landmark in your block. No matter how young your little girl may be, no matter how humble her specialties may seem, you will find that just knowing there is something in which she ex-

cels will do more for her morale than any planned incentive.
But you must set the stage.

She will need basic instruction in her specialty, and as much
special instruction as you can provide. She will perhaps want
books or magazines that pertain to her interest (turn a teenager loose with a copy of a really "gourmet" cookbook and
watch her interest soar).

But most important, you must provide her with honest encouragement and lavish praise.

Perhaps putting the teabags into the tea canister after every
marketing trip is your toddler's contribution to family life.
Perhaps your middle child will be in chage of keeping soap-
dishes filled with fresh bars of soap when required or changing
the roll of toilet tissue when the supply runs low. Perhaps, if
you are an apartment dweller, your daughter's gardening is
limited to watering the ivy and philodendron and keeping a
constant water supply on the narcissus bulbs in their dark
corner of the closet.

But whatever her specialty, she is learning the priceless lesson that no skill is humble. It is a glorious feeling to be able
to express the love we feel for others in something we've done
with our own hands, and every child will benefit by a taste of
that heady experience. For girls, nearly all of whom will grow
up to be full-time or part-time homemakers, that experience
is a necessary ingredient of growing up.

But to allow each girl to concentrate on the tasks at which
she is most competent is only one way of assuring that "helping around the house" will be meaningful.

Just as important as their efficiency in the skills and techniques of housework is the attitude they are developing toward
the job as a whole. The earlier we expose our youngsters to the
premise that housework need not be drudgery, the better our
chances of success, for to the very little girl all work is fun.

The right equipment can do wonders, too. An effective bait
for hooking young victims is the array of new chemical marvels

that shoot, swish, whoosh, and explode from various bomb-type containers. Or the window cleaners that change from a creamy liquid to a powdery coating, and the silicone polishes that go on like oil, then form an easily-wiped-away film. Small girls have fewer spills if, where the product or container permits, you pour into a saucer just the amount needed for the job. If your children are *very* small, spread these compounds yourself, then turn the helpers loose with an armful of clean cloths when you are ready to start polishing. Not only will they be kept happy and busy, but they do help—they really do. Of course you still have to give their windows a finishing up, but see if even a two-year-old doesn't cut your work time (and your fatigue) in half.

But perhaps you aren't interested in doing your present work in less time; you only wish, in the time you are now spending, that you could fit in a few more jobs. Child labor is the answer!

I'm a perfectionist about ironing—or rather I used to be and wish I could be again. But with each new baby a few more items were consigned to the rough-dry pile. Ah, but I've learned to take one eager eight-year-old, one automatic iron set very low, one adjustable ironing board (also set very low), and the result—tee shirts, plissé shorts, pajamas, etc., look the way they did when I started keeping house. It doesn't take her long, perhaps twenty minutes three times a week, but that's just one hour I never could seem to spare.

We surely don't save time on dishwashing, though. With all the giggling, splashing, and heart-to-heart talking we do, we take twice as long as we really should, but the dinner dishes at our house are the center of a beloved institution. When I was about thirteen, Mother and I spent one weekend each month with an aunt in a nearby suburb. For me those weekends were deadly dull until I volunteered—or perhaps someone suggested—that I help Molly with the dinner dishes.

Molly was the intriguing mystery woman who presided over Aunt Jane's kitchen. A teacher, they said she had been, but no one would say much more, and there was a fat, well-mannered, unexplained little boy that no one talked about either, who lived at home with Molly's mother. But regardless of her morals, or perhaps because she had learned compassion the hard way, Molly was a wise and understanding person. A big, frankly fat, laughing young woman, with curly black hair and Irish-blue eyes, she had a boundless store of anecdotes, parables, and good advice. She knew more about history and philosophy and psychology than anyone I had yet known; and I mean my relatives no disrespect, but the fact is that the talk in the kitchen was frequently several notches above the talk in the living room.

How I learned to look forward to those weekends! Was there an exam I was worried about? A boy who wouldn't call? An argument with Mother? Over the soapsuds in that big, old-fashioned kitchen somehow it all got straightened out. I vowed that if I ever had daughters we would always wash the dishes together, and we always—well, almost always—do. And just with one daughter at a time. They take turns helping me, exchanging turns freely when it's more convenient that way. Several times one of the girls has come home from school troubled and subdued, and before dinner I've heard a whispered conference in the hall, "Listen, let me do the dishes tonight, will you?" No one puts it into words, but we all understand.

In addition to problems you will find they bring up birds-and-bees questions at the kitchen sink. Apparently if there's something difficult to talk about, it's easier to be casual when your hands and eyes can busy themselves with a soapy cup or platter.

No, our girls don't consistently straighten their own rooms or even make their own beds (beds should air for most of the morning, I firmly believe). But they are always offering to "tidy up" the sewing basket, or clean the oven. Or I walk into the living room to find that someone has picked up the scattered Sunday paper without urging and without comment.

And when our daughters—and all daughters—carry a very real part of the housework load, they learn a rare and precious secret. They discover the joy of a room, aired and clean smelling, where sunlight pours through sparkling windows onto floors and furniture polished to a soft sheen by busy, loving hands; where each of us puts her hand to whatever task awaits her at the moment, and in the doing creates a *home*.

CHAPTER 5

So Many Ways to Be a Woman

According to Kipling,

> *There are ... something, something ... ways of*
> *constructing tribal lays,*
> *And every single one of them is right.*

I NEVER can remember how many ways he says there are, but I know this: however many there are, there are even more ways to be a woman. And every single one of them is right!

It has always seemed to me that this is one of the great joys of mothering little girls, this wide, wonderful freedom to encourage them to grow in any direction in which they naturally lean.

Boys have much less leeway. The world says "this is how a man must be," and every boy is then expected to bend his ways to suit the mold; then woe betide the understanding mother who encourages a sensitive, artistic boy to follow his own star.

Ah, but daughters are different! The world holds joy and fame and high approval in store for women of every type—the athlete, the go-getting businesswoman, the sensitive artist, the old-fashioned homebody.

If there is any pressure on a growing daughter to conform, it is more likely to arise within the home than in the world outside. And it is most apt to be brought to bear by the one person upon whose understanding she should be able to depend—her mother.

Sometimes the pressure is overt, as in the case of the little back-to-school shopper we discussed in Chapter 2. The tomboy forced to choose between nylon sheer ruffles and blue jeans—because she loves us and needs our love (how love can hang like a sword above a child!)—soon learns not to choose the jeans. Choosing them, she knows she loses stature in our eyes and that she cannot bear. But if she yields, she loses, too, for in her ruffly dress she's still not quite what we want—she knows it and we know it, too.

The fault is ours. We gave her an impossible choice: to be a second-rate girl or to be an imitation boy. When we over-simplify we overlook—and our daughters may never learn—the fact that there are many ways to be a woman.

Babe Didrikson Zaharias, the greatest woman athlete the world has ever watched, loved to cook and sew, was as talented with a needle and a frying pan as she was with a golf club, and anyone who read George Zaharias' tribute after her tragic death knows she was a total success as a friend, as a wife, as a woman. Apparently, when Babe was a little girl, no one ever bothered to tell her that nice little girls don't climb trees or play baseball or cowboys with the boys on the block. And since no one ever told her, she just developed according to her own healthy instincts, doing everything well and loving everything she did.

The tomboy takes first place in any discussion of patterns and molds and maternal pressures, because she is the one type of little girl who causes her mother real concern.

The bookworm or the junior scientist may be difficult for her mother to understand, but the tomboy's mother is more than baffled, she is worried.

She will say that she is afraid her child will be hurt, that her daughter is too hard on her clothes, that the noise of the gang of boys she runs with is deafening. But of course none of those is the reason she's trying to change her little girl. The real reason, though it may be hidden deep, is the uneasy knowledge that as a tomboy daughter grows older she walks a perilously narrow line between Mrs. Grundy's amused indulgence and her suspicious disapproval.

A really worried mother can save herself much anxiety by talking her fears over with her pediatrician, or with a counselor at a Child Guidance Clinic. But much needless worry springs from simple exaggeration. It is quite in the natural order of things for little girls and little boys to enjoy the same toys up to the age of five or six. Then their tastes begin to diverge, but it is a gradual process, far slower for some girls than for others. If, by the time she reaches puberty, a girl still shows definite resentment at her feminine role, selects clothes to minimize her newly developing contours, then it is advisable to seek out expert counsel.

But psychologists tell us such tragedies need not occur, if she is taught from her toddler years that it's fun to be a girl. Often, in our concern, we do just the opposite—everything she considers fun we label "out of bounds."

Without trying to make her over according to some mental image of our own, there are six constructive steps that we can take to make life happier for the tomboy who really goes to extremes:

1. Show her that life can be as exciting for a woman as for a man. Point out cases of feminine truck drivers, aviators, girls' baseball clubs; there's scarcely a job in the world, no matter how hard or how dangerous, that some woman somewhere isn't doing and doing well.

2. Take her where women are applauded and lionized. Plan an evening at a concert, if she loves music, when a feminine artist of rank is appearing. If she has an aunt or a family friend in the business world, perhaps a guided tour of her office or store would point up the importance of women in business. Give her a chance to see women of stature in as many fields as possible.

3. Ply her with biographies of exciting women, women who have lived lives of creativity and adventure; women such as Florence Nightingale, Margaret Bourke White, Eleanor Roosevelt, Madame Curie.

4. How is her relationshp with her dad? Is it man to man? In every way you can, encourage a father-daughter rather than father-son feeling. If Dad's taking her fishing, get her a bright tailored-yet-feminine outfit, a lunch box that's clearly meant for a little girl, a smart (rather than a farmer-type) straw hat. If he's taking her to a ball game perhaps he could suggest that she dress up a bit for the occasion and that they stop for ice cream somewhere afterward. Instead of concentrating on a shared interest in sports, he could teach her chess or checkers or simple card games she can play with girls as well as boys. A dad who notices his daughter's smart new dress, who brings her a feminine frill of talcum or toilet water or hand lotion now and then, who draws out her chair and opens doors and holds her coat as graciously as he does for her mother, can soften a tomboy almost single-handed.

5. Initiate her very early into your own feminine world, into all our mysterious rituals of beauty and make-up and manicures and hair-dos. Let her try her hand at some of the creative areas, not just the routine tasks, of cooking and dressmaking

(a pair of mother-daughter dresses would be a rewarding project).

Above all, stress the joy and wonder of the one job only we women can do. If motherhood is a shining thing to you, some of your satisfaction with your role will make itself felt eventually.

6. Wait. Wait without trying to change her (except for the constant struggle to keep her clean). Wait with the sure knowledge that one day she'll begin to emerge like a butterfly struggling out of its cocoon. The baseball stars will still be pasted to her walls, but now Pat Boone will be added. Soon you'll notice she wears her charm bracelet even to play stickball with the boys. And the boys change subtly, too. Where once they stood in the yard and bellowed, "Oh, Peg-gy," now they knock politely, their hair slicked back and their shirts tucked in. Your tomboy is becoming a woman. And here you'll have no shrill, brash, boy-crazy little flirt. For with her casual, easy friendliness born of years of playing with boys, with her quiet assumption that boys are people, and with her interest in their interests, this graceful new butterfly will be ready to soar into the social whirl with delightful, natural charm.

But not all pressures are overt; there are more subtle ways in which we influence our daughters to conform to our picture of what we want them to be.

In many—in fact, in most—homes the one child who does not conform to the majority pattern is considered automatically in the wrong, and is expected to change, though in a home across the street, where the pattern is a different one, that same little girl would be considered a model of perfection. It sometimes seems that the quiet, shy child is forever being nagged to be more like her friendly, outgoing sister, while every noisy, active child is forever being hushed.

Yet surely the extrovert daughter has a right to be an extrovert, while the introvert has a right to the peace and quiet she needs. Tick off your family members one by one: who are happiest when they are surrounded by people? Who are most content in a quiet world? You can work the most amazing change in the atmosphere of your home just by catering to the differences, by letting each child *be* the child she really is.

Take the quiet child first. If you're a peace person yourself you know what bothers her most—confusion, noise, people milling around, chatter, everyone talking at once. If these things don't bother you, you may have been underestimating the damage they can do.

On the other hand, it's nearly impossible for you, if you're a quiet person yourself, to comprehend how exhilarating another daughter may find the very atmosphere that drives you to distraction.

This type of tolerant understanding of differences is even more important to a daughter than it is to her brothers. Because a daughter spends so much more of her time at home, harmony in her home life is all-important.

Here are a few suggestions, some from child-guidance experts, some from other mothers of daughters, that will help create in your home a climate of acceptance where both the extrovert and the introvert daughter can feel equally secure.

Prescription for small extrovert. Even very tiny babies choose sides early. Such an outgoing little one likes toys hung on her crib, enough light at nap time to see well, a radio or phonograph providing background music all day long. While she's still nap-in-her-carriage age, a bright towel blowing on a clothesline above her will often keep her contented. Later she'll like her crib and her playpen set near a window that offers a view of passing cars and dogs and people. She'll love mobiles, Chinese wind chimes, bright primitive colors, and all her favorite toys will be noisy ones. Once she begins to talk she'll never stop, and if it drives you wild, you'll encourage her to bring friends home to play—an audience to "spell" you for a while. Nursery school can be a lifesaver, too, for both of you. Later, try to give her her own inexpensive radio or phonograph—she'll play it constantly and feel as though she has company even when she's alone. One friend who had two gregarious children sleeping in separate rooms moved them into the same bedroom, made the second bedroom a playroom for both, and reports that at last they're both willing to go to bed at night. Encourage doting aunts and uncles or grandparents to take your extrovert daughter on exciting jaunts, to the circus, downtown shopping, anywhere that offers bright lights, noise, and people.

Prescription for young introvert. Sudden noises startle the young introvert while she's very young, and continuing noise makes her nervous. She sleeps best in a quiet room with the shades drawn and the door closed. During her first few months, handle her with exaggeratedly slow and deliberate movements. This baby doesn't thrive on drive-in movies, picnics, carnivals, and block parties! As she grows older the introverted daughter needs a room of her own so much. If that is impossible, try to arrange a sun porch, alcove of the attic, some place where she can lock the door and be alone.

When she does join the family, make sure you listen to what she wants to say. Where there are several children, the quiet child can so easily be drowned out, and she won't fight to be heard as the others will; she'll just trail quietly off, feeling vaguely that *something* is wrong, and it must be she.

When it comes to dancing classes, Brownies, and all the inevitable girls' clubs in and out of school, try not to push her into joining; at least, try not to push her more than just a little (she needs a *little* push, this quiet one).

There's a limit to how much peace is possible in a home with several children, but we stumbled onto a useful device—the bathtub. Early in the evening the younger two splash their noisy way through a shared bath, are bundled into sleepers, and sent into the living room to watch television or hear a story. Meanwhile Lindy, who likes to be alone, draws a deep, warm tub of bubble bath (we use dishwashing detergent; it is cheaper, smells just as good, and soaks off the grime). I lay out her pajamas and turn off the overhead light, leaving on just the dim night light, and she is free to loll and float and scrub and stretch and meditate until the younger children go to bed, if she likes.

When a child finds that her home is geared to her needs in this way, she knows you have accepted her as the person she really is. And a child who's accepted wholly as she is gains such a triumphant feeling of worth and value. In this warm awareness of her own merit she can meet the world on equal terms, neither bowing nor battling for her place. In your acceptance (and for a child your acceptance is tantamount to the world's) she finds self-respect.

This calm acceptance of the fact that there are many ways to be a woman will help you conquer that bogey of child rearing, favoritism. Parents who are sure of themselves and their roles, who understand their daughters' differing traits and differing needs, are well aware that they love each child in a different way. That's not favoritism, that's common sense.

This whole business of favoritism is a ticklish one to most parents. We somehow feel that we should love in carefully measured packages, and when one child irritates us, or when her chatter bores us, then surely we are failures as parents.

If you have felt that way sometimes—and if you have more than one child then you surely have—you may be reassured by what Dr. Spock has had to say on the subject. He maintains that to love our children means two things: to cherish them and to enjoy them. If we cherish one child above another, if we sacrifice the other children's welfare for hers, that is wrong. The standard test is that old, old dilemma: if your children were trapped in a fire or a shipwreck and you could save only one, which would you rescue? If the answer is there waiting for you instantly, then you need the help of a family counselor or a child-guidance expert. For to cherish one child more than another is inexorably wrong.

But enjoyment—ah, that's another matter. There are some people, adults, strangers, or acquaintances, for whom we feel little warmth. We simply are not so comfortable with them as with other people. It's inevitable that there are children, delightful children, perhaps, who are so very different from ourselves that we just don't particularly enjoy their company. And sometimes they're our own. Dr. Spock assures us we wouldn't be human if it were otherwise.

Fortunately, it's often an age we're allergic to, not the individual child. Many women get very little satisfaction from the first three months of a baby's life. I know other mothers who dread that fifth year when so often a child's baby cuteness and baby teeth vanish simultaneously.

But inevitable as it is that there are some types of women a mother admires more than others, nevertheless she is inviting sorrow if she tries to force her daughter into the approved mold.

Now I don't propose for a moment that we abdicate our responsibility when we agree that there are many ways to be a woman. We must still weed out all the traits that don't belong and plant and tend the admirable ones. But we would be wise to do it carefully, sparingly, as a skilled gardener prunes a shrub to bring out its symmetry and encourage its flowering, but never tries to disguise it as a different species.

For even if the pressures exerted on a child to shape her to a mother's pattern are so subtle that they create little unhappiness during her childhood, they may be the source of serious conflicts after she becomes an adult, if life should demand of her a different role from the one her mother envisioned.

She may have been brought up to believe that women are gentle and submissive, only to have the death of her husband or a disabling accident catapult her into the role of "man of the house." Or years of emphasis by her mother on dignity, formality, and reserve may ill prepare her for marriage to a dashing, unconventional character who expects her to entertain all sorts of odd types at all sorts of odd hours and catch a plane for the Coast on an hour's notice.

It's not that she won't rise to the occasion; since human beings are as adaptable as they are, she'll meet the test. But if her mother spent twenty years indoctrinating her with the theory that *this* is how a woman is and a woman who doesn't fit the pattern is a failure or a freak, she's not going to be happy about her new role. She'll be plagued by self-pity, or guilt. Or she'll discover that there *are* fine women who don't live according to her mother's specifications, and then she will turn cynical about *all* the standards and ideals her mother taught her.

Speaking of guilt, let's talk about us for a moment. This kindly acceptance must be a two-way proposition. Children—and girls seem to be the worst offenders—expect a mother to be all things. They are proud if she's a successful businesswoman, but they feel she ought to have time to bake brownies for the Christmas party. They like her to be home when they get home, receptive to the latest school news, ready to sew on a button or press a blouse; yet they can't understand why she gave up her music, when it would be such fun to have a glamorous concert artist for a mother!

When I was in grade school, I often thought how happy I would be if my mother were like Ernestine's. A plump, jolly woman with a love for good cooking and all children, she often invited me over for the most delicious lunches. Or like Harriet's mother—whenever it rained unexpectedly, she'd appear at the door with Harriet's raincoat and rubbers. My mother, busy at her office job, wasn't that available.

Yet when there was a P.T.A. meeting, I'd look around at the plain, slightly dowdy, slightly dumpy mothers of many of my schoolmates, and contrast them with the beautiful, sleek, sophisticated mother I had brought, and I'd nearly burst with pride and love.

Most children are like that, I think. They must be told that in this as in any other area they cannot eat their cake and have it, too.

Though family life conspires to make us forget it, we are women as well as mothers, and each of us has a right—indeed has a duty—to *be* the kind of woman we are inside.

If working at a job outside our home seems necessary to us, then we make the decision, that's all. If we are homebodies at heart, no snide remarks about new bicycles or water skis should make us feel guilty for not supplementing the family income.

No matter what life you choose to live, your children will think that they have some regrets, and you'll never be sure you did the right thing anyway. But at least you'll have lived your own life and had fun along the way. There's nothing more pathetic than an aging woman who bent her life first to her parents' demands, then to her husband's, and then to her children's, and never did have a year of her life to herself.

So live a little! There's nothing like an offbeat hobby, or one foolish extravagance (fabulous perfume, perhaps, or camellias, or first editions) to make our children see us as somebody special.

If you would rather spend the summer days creating a beautiful garden than to stay inside baking cupcakes, do it.

If you think being thin as a fashion model is foolish, stop apologizing for your weight, relax, and make the most of yourself just the way you are. When your daughters nag you to diet, point out television's glamorous Virginia Graham, who's frankly heavy by high fashion standards, but as beautiful as any woman in show business. Of course, if you're going to cite her as an example, you'll have to emulate her, and make even more effort than a slender woman to insure that you're flatteringly coiffed, smartly dressed, faultlessly groomed.

Or if you want to hire a housekeeper and break into politics, and your husband thinks it's a fine idea, too—do it. The children may complain, but in the long run they'll gain as much as they'll lose, and they'll respect you for your independence.

It's so easy for motherhood to become all giving and no getting; that's what breeds martyrdom and self-pity. But if it works both ways, if our families realize that there are many ways to be a mother, it's lots easier for us to be understanding about our children's differing aims and goals.

And their instincts for the right aims and goals are often surprisingly perceptive. When we differ with our daughter about the woman she wishes to become, there is just the bare possibility that *we* might be wrong. As we grow older our values shift and mature; tomorrow we may see our daughters differently. The scatterbrained little chatterbox whose flightiness is our despair today, tomorrow may seem a shining light in this humdrum world. The studious solemn daughter who today seems so graceless and dull, tomorrow may change the world with a contribution so vast it dwarfs our dreams for her.

The world is cruel to the people it labels odd, but the world takes us pretty much at our own evaluation, lets us to a large degree write our own labels. We can best help our daughters win the world's acceptance by bringing them up with the happy assurance that there are countless different ways to be a woman—and the confidence that "every single one of them is right."

CHAPTER 6

Give Her a Father

Put Father back at the head of the family," the sociologists, jurists, psychiatrists—just about all the experts—are shouting. Well, whoever said we mothers wanted it any other way?

We can't pick up a magazine that doesn't feature an article deploring the Decline of Father, or declaring that the situation comedies on radio and television, with their weak, bumbling male leads, depict the decay of American home life. I've never talked with a woman who enjoyed being the head of the house, though some of them admittedly were.

It would seem that Mother, Father, and the experts all agree on where Dad should be but no one is quite sure how to get him back there. And the confusion is compounded when the family he's supposed to head is composed of girls.

I recently read of an obstretician who has two different fee schedules, one for the fathers whose first words were "Is it a boy or a girl?" and a considerably lower one for the "Are they both all right, Doctor?" breed. There are fathers, I'm told—and though I've never met one, I believe it—who simply cannot accept a baby girl. Obviously such a man is sick, with the roots of his conflicts so deep that he urgently needs psychiatric help.

But there are other fathers, men who love their little girls dearly, who honestly believe that there's very little a father and daughter can do together. Being pals with a child means hunting and fishing to such a man, nothing else but hunting and fishing, and possibly the Little League. What he needs is an education, and we mothers are just the girls to educate him!

Most of us realize that a daughter's attitude toward her father will shape her outlook toward other men, herself, her mother, and life.

What most of us do *not* realize is that a daughter's attitude toward her father is shaped by her mother.

We alone, for instance, can see to it that they spend time together, both alone and as a family.

Every neighborhood has one family whose children stand out as models of good adjustment and healthy, wholesome attitudes. The one on our street that instantly comes to mind consists of two little girls, four and eight, and a boy ten, handsome, well-behaved, obviously happy youngsters. And the very factor that has molded them is a situation most family experts would deplore—their father works all day and their mother works at night. But here is a father who really knows his children, who spends hours each day in close companionship with them, who doesn't base his opinions of their capabilities and their problems on second-hand reports.

We can set the stage for such a relationship without joining the night shift. We can start by handing over the responsibility for a very young baby girl to her dad for an evening now and then. You will note that I said "responsibility." It is amazing how we lose sight of the fact that a man capable of driving a bus, operating a crane hoist, or supervising five hundred men, surely can cope with one little baby for three or four hours. By the time we've dashed around leaving lists, warnings, instructions, timetables, and charts, it's no wonder our husbands feel that the whole idea is a chore and an imposition. At least it certainly isn't fun. A bottle and a pile of diapers, that's all the equipment he needs.

That principle of simplification goes for any outing with the baby, too. If a husband's suggestion of a Sunday-afternoon ride is met with frantic scurrying to corral all the baby paraphernalia, and two or three trips to the car to stow it all away, his invitations will be few and far between. But what a difference if there is a diaper bag kept ready, stocked with a few clean diapers, a teething biscuit or some zwieback, perhaps, always one extra bottle made up in the refrigerator, and your young lady's outer garments all in one place. Not only will a father act on his impulse more often, but he'll be convinced that you're the cleverest, most efficient young mother in the block.

I know whereof I speak, for I've been the world's worst offender in this area for years. How I envy women who can be ready to pick up and go on a moment's notice! I'm improving, though; I'm improving simply because years of observation have convinced me that the women who do things on the spur of the moment, children or no children, who can change plans with very little notice, are the women who enjoy the most fun with their families and promote the most "togetherness" between father and daughter.

One of our neighbors has developed a wonderfully efficient approach to summer picnics and outings. Every marketing day during the summer she buys the nucleus of a picnic lunch— chicken for frying or a package each of frankfurters and buns, a can or two of lemonade, fresh fruit, "bought" cookies. These are tucked away either in the picnic basket or at the back of the freezer or refrigerator, all in one spot, along with a half-dozen hard-boiled eggs. Before the weekend the picnic basket is checked. Are napkins, paper plates and cups, salt, can opener all ready? And, if it's swimming weather, are all the bathing suits, caps, a towel apiece, and the sun-tan oil all in one place? Then, if Saturday or Sunday dawn brilliant and beckoning, ten minutes—literally—is all they need to get under way. But all the planning has been so inconspicuous that if it rains or her husband just doesn't feel like fighting the traffic, he needn't feel guilty, the children aren't disappointed, and everything can be served for the girls' lunches or saved until the next weekend. Or she may let the children have a picnic in the back yard, while she and her husband dine alone in unaccustomed peace and quiet in the dining room or at a card table on the cool front porch.

Yet such idyllic situations are not universal. The weekend is a source of conflict in a surprising number of homes. And I'm convinced it's a problem we women often create for ourselves. I suspect that a close look at our motives would make us squirm.

We say, "The children need their father," and we believe it. But don't we really mean, "A man's place is home with us on Sundays?" And who taught us that? Why, our own mothers.

When an unhappy woman sees her husband driving off to the golf links on a weekend, or loading his fishing gear into the trunk, she may really be seeing a vision of her mother (or her sister-in-law, or her best friend) watching with raised eyebrows and pursed lips, plainly thinking, "Humpf! If *my* husband cared so little about his family ...." Honestly, now, isn't that true?

When we vowed we were forsaking all others, that included old ways, old standards, even, perhaps, old traditions. How many Christmas Eves, how many Christmas mornings, have been spoiled because we somehow assume that the holiday traditions we were raised in are the "right" traditions.

There is something in many of us that welcomes martyr-dom, that craves and feeds upon self-pity. We take some care-less, thoughtless gesture (aren't we occasionally careless and thoughtless, too?) and we brood upon it, nurse it, rehearse speeches we will never make, build up the incident to the children, until it becomes a test, a battle of wills. And the children are the losers.

That's bad enough; what's unforgivable is that it's so often not what he wants to do vs. what we want, as it is what he wants to do vs. what we feel is expected of us both. Let's have the courage to break the pattern! Let's decide right now that this is a new family unit, creating a whole new body of tradition, gradually working out by trial and error a pattern of living that suits us as a family. We will be offering our daughters a fine example for their own marriages.

For years I cooked a big Sunday dinner. I spent hours over it, seething inside all the while because I knew what would happen. My husband would hopefully suggest driving somewhere, or going for a walk, and I'd say well, not right now, dinner won't be ready until one, and then he would look resigned and disappointed, and he'd settle down with the Sunday paper. After dinner there were all those dishes to wash. By two-thirty I was ready to go, but by then it was naptime for the baby. By the time she woke it was too late. How I came to hate Sundays!

Then one day I faced the fact that just because my mother served a big Sunday dinner didn't mean it was right for us. Stubborn though I am, I've tried to work out a happier solution. Now we have a very light breakfast before church, just cereal, fruit juice, and cocoa, usually. For after church I plan a hearty brunch, with sausage or chip steaks, eggs, fruit and a homemade hot bread to make the meal special. It takes only a little time to fix, and a whole day is lying there waiting for us when we are through. Or, now that nothing is waiting in the oven, if the leaves are turning scarlet in Delaware Park, we may be tempted to stop on the way home from church and spend an hour feeding acorns to the squirrels or skipping stones in the lake. If it's a lazy day when we've skipped church entirely, we may eat in our robes, carrying the brunch on trays to the living room.

One of our friends solved the problem of golf widowhood by the same sort of honest reappraisal. She came to realize that it really wasn't the children's lack of companionship with their Daddy that bothered her—she just wanted him home on Sundays. Once she faced that fact, she turned her attention to finding new ways to make it a happy day for the children. At first she packed a picnic lunch and asked her husband to take them along to the park next to the golf course. Those first weeks it was awfully hard not to alternate between self-righteousness and self-pity, but soon the children and she accepted this as the new way of weekends. Then her husband and his partners took to walking down the slope to the picnic area for a sandwich and coffee before going on to the back nine. Soon a second wife liked the idea and with another family along the day was twice as much fun. Now that she was no longer fighting for a cause, the whole tenor of their weekends changed. Even husbands who are enthusiastic family men may have a better time when we invite another couple to go along.

Then one Sunday morning my friend asked herself why they were driving all that way to the picnic grounds and back, when they had a pleasant back yard, equipped with a barbecue grill and a plastic wading pool. Now nearly every summer Sunday you will find a picnic in progress in their back yard, often with two or three other families. And the men, tired and happy, not only get home just as fast as they can after the game, they've taken to starting out earlier in the morning so they can spend Sunday with their families. But this was more than a happy compromise for a golf widow's dilemma; it was an example of how well we can work out ways for our daughters to have more time with their dads if we think constructively, not emotionally.

So much for summer. But even the most devoted family man bogs down at the thought of winter.

Now, nothing sounds cozier than a winter Sunday spent at home. It conjures up a picture of checkers and mulled cider before a blazing log fire. But it doesn't work out quite that way in our little corner of Suburbia, and I'm sure we are not alone. Call ten friends any February day and ask them how they spent last Sunday afternoon and eight of the families will sigh that they didn't set foot out of the house. At least that was what happened in our limited sampling. And more dispirited, dreary voices you never heard. All eight families had the same complaint—too many people, especially little people, cooped up together for too many months—that February rut.

What in the world can you do with February?

What can you do with it? Why, you can plan outings, go places, see things, have *fun!* It isn't necessary to waste the whole end of winter marking time until spring; you can decide to enjoy February—and March, too—no matter what the weather, and find that you are happier, healthier, and know more—more about your town, about the surrounding farm lands, about that vast body of knowledge lumped together under the title of Nature.

Of the three ways to have winter fun, you undoubtedly have tried two: winter sports and indoor activities. But for many families with small daughters both have serious limitations. Skiing, skating, and tobaganning all presuppose a family of school-age children, or none at all. For the young couple with a toddler, an infant, and perhaps another on the way, strenuous winter sports are not the answer.

Well, then, let's consider the second type of winter adventure, the things we can do indoors. Visits to museums, art galleries, hobby exhibits can be valuable and pleasurable, and throughout the country YMCA's and community centers offer classes in everything from archery to zither playing, with babysitting provisions thrown in. But staying indoors is avoiding winter, not enjoying it. So let's turn to the third type of activity: discover the unexpected charm of our favorite summer haunts revisited.

To most people the idea of a trip to the beach or a picnic in the park in February comes as a shock, but if you try it once you will become an enthusiastic booster of winter outings.

Let's start with a not-too-daring expedition close to home. Have you ever taken the children to the zoo in the winter? Oh, yes, it's open. And it is unbelievably still and wild, as different from the summertime zoo as Cape Cod is from Coney Island. Now there are no souvenir stands, no hot-dog carts. If it is a large zoo, as ours is, you can walk for an hour without meeting another human. It seems so deserted that I was amazed when Mr. Joseph Abgott, curator of the Buffalo, New York, zoo, told me that even on really stormy weekends there are several hundred visitors, while a sunny, beautiful Sunday in late winter may bring ten to twelve thousand people. Yet, in contrast to the summer crowds (45,000 visitors in the biggest single day last summer!) it is deserted.

Naturally, some of the animals have been moved inside. The monkeys have retired to the comfort of the monkey house and the zebras and ostriches need a heated shelter. But many animals that are dull and lethargic in summer heat (the yaks, for instance, most of the bears, all the varieties of deer, and oddly enough the camels) become vigorous and alert when the temperature drops. Such crowd-shy species as the deer, rabbits, and foxes relax and romp in the security of the off-season solitude.

Rules are relaxed, too, and doors marked "No Admission" swing open literally and figuratively. Perhaps you will be allowed to watch, as we did, eight vivid screaming macaws being crated, much against their will, for shipment to a distant zoo.

Or a keeper may beckon to the children to push open the door they have been peeking through, and learn how he prepares the meat for the lions' lunch. Our children still talk about the tiny white mouse who hopped onto the food cart when his cage was opened, rode along, eating all the while, as the cart rolled from cage to cage, the length of the whole corridor and back, then leaped into his own cubicle again at a command from the attendant.

But the zoo is only the beginning. What else do you enjoy in the summer that you can transplant into this snowy month?

Well, how about a picnic? Some of our friends who are rugged outdoor souls drive to a nearby state park and make a whole day of it, but they don't recommend it to anyone who is not an experienced and skilled woodsman. Though most state and county parks are not closed to the public during the winter, in most cases the parking lots and shelters are unattended, and a stalled car, a sudden storm, a child who wanders out of sight could hold the seeds of tragedy. An easy way to get an expert's advice about your local situation is to drop a line or make a call to your state or county park commission.

Being less hardy folk, we frequent the city parks, sometimes alone, often with another family. It may be the climax to a day of sledding with the youngsters, or, when the children are very small, the main event. Either way, a winter picnic is delightful! As with any outing, a little advance planning insures success.

In planning the food, something hot and hearty is important. An easy cooked-and-ready meal consists of a pot of bubbling hot beans carried in an insulated container. Cooked hamburgers can be placed right on the beans, and buttered buns tucked alongside. With this children like hot tomato soup from a thermos. Cookies and fruit, the traditional picnic dessert, can serve as a snack if everyone gets too hungry before you reach your destination.

If you know there will be cooking facilities, you might take wieners or hamburgers for the meat course. A big thermos of hot soup belongs in this menu, too, and for dessert a box of marshmallows to toast over the fire.

Remember how you worried about the baby's formula souring during summer picnics? Now, the whole outdoors is your cooler, and when you're ready, there are clever warmers that plug into the dashboard lighter.

For everyone from the baby to you warm clothes, or, more accurately, several layers of light, waterproof clothes are vital. The Boy Scout and Girl Scout handbooks have excellent suggestions for dressing for warmth-without-bulk on hikes. In addition, a good rule to follow is: *Boots on the children no matter what the weather.*

The mothers we know agree that toddlers should be diapered for outings such as these, even though they are toilet-trained in normal situations. Not one of us has ever had any trouble with a child becoming confused by this inconsistency. Apparently children of this age have more sense than we sometimes give them credit for—they recognize an exception when confronted with one.

When our Joyce was still in diapers I used a new diaper liner on these outings which by some mixture of black magic and modern chemistry lets the moisture pass through to the diaper and then keeps it there; in a few minutes the baby's skin is entirely dry and stays that way. The trade name is Dryper, and you can find them at most department stores and baby shops.

Being dry is the key to being warm you will find. It's a sensible precaution to keep a turkish towel and several pairs of Dad's out-worn wool socks in the car for the drive back home.

The timing of that drive back home is important; this is not the time of year for an all-day outing if your children are small. The timetable that works best for us is to leave early and return early enough to give the children a light snack and a warm bath before bedtime.

We do make one exception to this schedule each season— our winter beach party. We try to choose a dry, clear, mild night. We leave little Joyce with a sitter and have a very early dinner so that a half-hour drive brings us to the lake shore at dusk.

While their father builds the fire with wood we've brought in the car, the girls and I sit on an old quilt, wrapped in blankets, offering advice. The darkness deepens swiftly this time of year, and the stars are there quite suddenly, all at once. It's bitterly cold by the lake on a winter night, but by the blazing fire we toast our marshmallows and sip our cocoa in complete comfort.

Of course you don't need so dramatic a setting as a lake shore by starlight. The park you loved last August becomes a whole new world now. The swings and slides are probably dismantled, but children will find exciting possibilities in a shelter packed to the rafters with tables and benches. There are trees to climb, too, and the heady wonder of all that space.

The grills and ovens will be as efficient as they were last summer, if you take the trouble to bring your own dry wood. Charcoal will do as well for cooking, of course, but winter picnics seem to call for the cheer and warmth of a high, blazing fire.

Plan to take along a bag of peanuts for the squirrels and chipmunks. Now, with their own larders depleted, these little fellows are amazingly ready to make friends. Clarence J. Hylander's book, *Outdoors in Winter*, adds a great deal of meaning to the sights you see, and we often include a pair of binoculars and a good bird book. The birds stand out clearly among the bare branches, and identification is much easier than during the leafy months.

That is part of the charm of these winter outings—the dramatic contrast of one brilliant flash of color against a background of black and white and grays. Even a very young child thrills to a scarlet cardinal in a gray tree against a gray sky, or to a bittersweet vine blazing on a rail fence.

Even total absence of color can be beautiful; a visit to a locally-famed scenic spot after a snowfall can be a breathtaking experience. One of our friends who is a camera enthusiast takes his family to Niagara Falls each winter and spends hours find-

ing new angles to photograph, while his children revel in the
sheath of ice that coats every fence, twig, and grass blade, and
splinters at a touch with the sound of shattering glass that is
very soul-satisfying to the young. There are dozens of lesser-
known points of interest at your doorstep.

Within a few miles from your city is bound to be a farm, a
wonderful destination for a father and daughter on a winter
day. Show me the father who doesn't believe he's a farm boy at
heart! This month is maple-syrup time for farmers in many
parts of the country, and gathering the sap is an educational
experience the whole family will enjoy. Or, if you're a hunting
widow, perhaps you'll enjoy sitting around the kitchen table
drinking coffee and talking woman talk while the men are off
hunting and the children are in the barn, watching the milking
or just jumping in the hay. If you don't know anyone who
owns a farm, you can get a brochure with detailed descriptions
of nearly three hundred farms in twenty-eight states and
Canada, who have provisions for guests for a day or longer.
Just send twenty-five cents to Farm Vacations and Holidays,
500 Fifth Avenue, New York 36, New York.

Or, instead of branching outward, you can head for downtown. Here's an area of the city where a man can really shine
in his daughter's eyes. A logical place to start your sight-seeing
is with a visit to the upper floor of your town's highest office
building. Sometimes this must be arranged in advance with the
building management, but it is well worth the small trouble
of a telephone inquiry. Now, without summer foliage, the pattern of streets and buildings stretches beneath you as sharply
as a map. Often children have a very vague conception of the
spatial relationship of school, church, Daddy's office, etc. It is
a real revelation to most youngsters to see their town from a
height.

The downtown area offers another treat for the small fry—
the department-store windows, especially in December. Most

fathers much prefer this arrangement to that dreadful excursion through the toy floor to Santa's throne. The Sunday before Christmas you can tour, in real solitude, the fabulous animated holiday windows, then two or three months later they are almost as enticing, with the glowing colors of new spring merchandise bringing a preview of Easter.

Now let's walk a few blocks farther, down toward the river, a spot that can yield several fascinating afternoons. One time Dad may offer to take them alone, which for the children will make the trip special. Perhaps your town has a colony of ice fishermen, those hardy souls who build a "village" of tents and shacks on the ice as a headquarters for their fishing. Since our city is a shipping center, we sometimes walk down to the docks, where the river boats are waiting out the winter. There is an old watchman there we love to talk with, a character out of a Burl Ives' folk song, who entertains the children with stories of his childhood as a barge boy on the Erie Canal.

When it gets late we walk back to the drugstore at the end of the street. While their dad goes back for the car, the children and I have mugs of hot chocolate, and by the time he picks us up, the car is warm inside, and so are we. Off come the children's boots, shoes, and socks, then a quick hard rub with the towel, and each girl slips her cold feet into a pair of big wool socks.

Finally, with the car robe tucked around their legs, their cheeks scarlet from the cold, little Joyce promptly falls asleep, while the older girls just relax, warm and happy, and feeling very, very close to us both.

But children don't need whole days with their fathers. It's the quality of their time together, not the quantity, that matters. If we use ingenuity and a little feminine trickery, every day can hold a little time for our girls to be with their fathers.

Let's look at the small baby's schedule first. For all our noble sentiments, we women are sometimes unreasonably resistant about shaping Baby's day around our husband's. Just putting her to bed an hour later or getting her up an hour earlier can make all the difference. And a half-hour of Father's undivided attention at bedtime is worth a whole day spent at a beach or being pushed in her buggy through the zoo, when the time is measured in closeness and warmth of feeling.

Most men enjoy overseeing bath time once a baby can sit alone in the big tub. Most fathers are terrific bedtime story-tellers, too, much preferring the creative approach rather than reading a book aloud.

Two words of caution though. First—leave them alone! True, her hair may get wet, the sleeper pants may be put on backward the first time. But this bath isn't to get her clean, it's to get her acquainted, so don't make her dad just an assistant mother who must do everything your way.

Second—remember that dads are different, too. One father may look forward all the way home to his romp with the youngsters before dinner. Another man might prefer not coming home at all to facing that. If your husband is unhappy in the nursery, accept him as he is. Just be sure it isn't because of lack of encouragement on your part.

If he comes home brutally tired at night, you won't stunt your child's emotional growth by requiring her to move and speak softly and seldom. On the contrary, you are teaching her a gentle consideration for the demands of a man's work, and that training will make her a better wife and mother someday.

A wonderful starting place is sending her along when your husband has to go out anyway on some small errand. Is he walking over to the drugstore for a pack of cigarettes? Try, "Why don't you take Debby along, dear? She'd love it." You might even imply that it would be a big favor to you, since you could give your whole attention to dinner. Before you know it, she'll be tagging along when he takes the car to the garage, or drives over to the lumberyard.

I mentioned feminine trickery; I'm going to pass along a trick of the trade I had to learn the hard way: the way a child looks when her father is ready to leave the house often determines whether or not she'll go along. I don't think fathers assess their daughters' appearance consciously, but you'll find that five minutes with a hairbrush and a soapy washcloth *before*, not *after*, you make the suggestion will increase her chances of a spur-of-the-moment invitation to tag along. The same sort of psychology lies behind the trick of having her outside in the winter. As soon as your husband announces that he'll have to take the washers back to the hardware store and get larger ones, you dash for the snowsuit, explaining that it's such a nice day to play in the yard. You bundle her up and help her out the door. Then, as long as Debby's already outside, in her snowsuit and all, why not take her along? Underhanded, yes, but effective.

And here's where those beautiful manners will prove their worth. The first time those two venture forth alone will be in the nature of an experiment. If that first tentative trial run goes smoothly, if Daddy's girl is quiet and poised and well behaved, she'll be asked again, you can be sure of that.

When that happens, you'll encounter a fascinating phenomenon: suddenly your husband discovers that his daughter isn't a baby any more. All these months you've been recounting tales of the progress she's made, the words she's mastered, but none of it really got through enough to change his mental image of her as an infant. Now *you* must listen to the clever things she said, the grown-up remark that surprised him so. I've always believed that the reason many fathers shelter their daughters fanatically, the reason they insist upon treating teenagers like little girls, is that they've spent too little time with their daughters to know their capabilities.

On the other hand, time spent with Dad can boost those capabilities considerably. There are so many areas of a child's life where her father is the logical mentor.

To a child just discovering the exciting door marked geography a father's overseas army reminiscences can open whole new worlds. *Your* contribution might be to serve a whole meal of exotic dishes of the foreign country under discussion.

Charles Van Doren, the young man who caught the fancy of a whole nation when his remarkable mind was spotlighted on a television quiz show, attributes his broad knowledge to one factor—his father's distinguished friends, who peopled his youth with important ideas and stimulating conversation. Many, many a man has equally eminent coworkers and friends; whether or not he brings them home where they can enrich a daughter's life depends almost entirely upon his wife—on the atmosphere and appearance of their home, on the quiet dignity of her hospitality, on the behavior of their children.

But the most run-of-the-mill young clerk can enrich the lives of his children just as much as a philosopher, an educator, or a statesman. He has only to understand that his role is to orient his girls with the world outside.

A visit to Daddy's office is one obvious suggestion, but there are countless other doors he can open for them. Science, perhaps, if that is his interest, for even such elementary activities as flying kites or catching and observing grasshoppers become fascinating experiments with a father who has a scientific bent.

The father who is a fan of any spectator sport provides his daughter with more than companionship when he takes her along to the stadium or the ball park; he's smoothing her path when, as a teenager, a talking acquaintance with her dates' interests will be a boon.

The handyman may welcome help as the girls reach hammer-holding age, or he may simply tolerate their presence. But even if he only teaches them the rudiments of routine household repairs he will be molding them into thrifty and self-sufficient wives. Fortunately the shifting sociological trends are on your side; just when you want your husband and daughter to have a hobby in common, the do-it-yourself philosophy makes carpentry for the girls not only practical but fashionable.

Nearly everybody once played a musical instrument. Find out your husband's youthful specialty and encourage him to take it up again when his daughter starts music lessons. Better yet—make it a trio.

Helping with homework isn't the only way a dad can help with school problems.

A father who takes an active part in P.T.A. and school board activities attains towering stature in his daughter's eyes. Most youngsters attach tremendous importance to anything connected with school: Dad's signature on their report cards, his attendance at open-house evenings. It's natural enough, since school and home are the twin poles of a daughter's world, that she should need to feel there is complete harmony between them.

But fathers can enlarge the world of little girls to include more than home and school. They can reach back into the past to introduce their daughters to history. Not dusty stories filled with dates and data, but stories and legends from local history, or sight-seeing trips to nearby historical shrines. You can do your bit to encourage them, if you see they are interested, by providing such props as descriptive literature of historical spots of interest, or appropriate records ("The Living Constitution" is an excellent addition to any home record library) and books. Or you might decide to subscribe to the magazine of history, *American Heritage.*

Or your husband may be a man more at home in the future, active in politics or in neighborhood improvement groups. At a surprisingly early age children respond to the color and excitement of a political campaign. You might send for the *Election Bulletin of the League of Women Voters* (non-partisan profiles of the candidates, with their own answers to a group of pertinent questions) to stimulate a father-daughter study and discussion session.

Of course there's more to government than just elections. The League of Women Voters can help there, too, through a little book outlining the offices of your city government, the qualifications for office, the salary, the staff of each department or agency, and much, much more. There's one for your town or city, if it boasts a League of Women Voters' branch. The booklet is technical, and requires adult interpretation, but it's fascinating. It may beguile your husband into taking his daughter to attend a city council meeting at city hall. And the interest you are now stimulating will build women who will take their civic privileges and responsibilities seriously.

If neither the past nor the future appeals to the father in your house, how about the present? The immediate and pressing problem of earning a living and making that living stretch across a whole month may strike the man who's mired in it as being pretty prosaic. But to a child the whole world of commerce and finance is a thrilling mystery. To a toddler, just visiting Dad's office is enough; a school-age youngster is ready to hear what the firm produces, where the raw materials originate, how the finished product is distributed and sold. This isn't just to provide him with an education in economics, it's to help him see his father's place—an important place, no matter what the job—in the world of men.

Like every other American youngster, our girls had heard the term "strike" all their lives, but when the union at the plant where their father works walked out last year, we found that the children had no idea at all what we were talking about. So one Saturday morning my husband walked up to the plant with the two older girls. They saw the placards, talked with some of the pickets, and learned in simplified, general terms the issues behind the srtike. That was a more telling lesson in economics than several periods spent in civics class.

In addition to understanding how money is earned, girls, particularly, as future managers of the household budget, need to learn how money is spent, and that's another area of living where a father's viewpoint is vital.

Though I understand many parents get this information across without giving their daughters any money-managing experience at all, I can't see how. A girl needs a set amount of money every week, no matter how small, which is hers, inviolate, with no strings attached. She also needs, once she has reached an age of discretion and can be trusted not to relay the details for the neighbors' edification, experience in planning and carrying out the family budget.

If parents fail in their children's money training it's not for lack of help. There are dozens of good books available on the subject at your library. And as good as the best of these is a little pamphlet called *Children's Spending*, which is available free at Household Finance Corporation offices all across the country. The school banking system is another valuable aid to thrift and a springboard for a father's explanation of the place of banks in our lives. No school bank? Suggest that your husband take her to the bank he frequents, making it a real occasion, fraught with drama and dignity. (Further along, in Chapter 15, there's a whole section on the part you can play in initiating your child into responsibility for the family's finances.)

As firm advocates of the family council system of home government, we thresh out allowance problems, as well as all other major issues, around the dining-room table during council meeting. We feel that much more is at stake here than just resolving the issues. The family council is really an end in itself, for here children experience their first brush with representative government. They learn their first hard lessons about yielding the floor, about majority rule, about orderly procedure of law. If you haven't tried the Great Experiment at your house, I urge you to send for *How to Hold a Family Council*, and give the booklet to your husband. Here is a project most fathers approve on sight.

There! That's the end of my list of suggestions. But it's just possible that your husband might have some excellent ideas of his own. That's a basic feminine inconsistency—isn't it?—that we want our husbands to take more interest in raising their daughters, yet when they proffer an idea we throw up a quick, reflex wall of resistance; surely I'm not the only one who does that. Yet looking back I can see that some of the most rewarding ideas we've tried have come from the father in our house, once I stopped being on the defensive about suggestions. Fathers—just because they haven't spent so many, many hours with their daughters—frequently bring a fresh objective outlook to the home scene.

If nothing else, they can inject a note of simple honesty into family relations. Psychologists, listing the traits in which men and women differ most, always mention the subtle, subjective, devious approach of women. And of course that's true. We're a great sex for hinting, for "managing." If a close relationship with her dad can help a girl to understand a man's need to be *told* what she's thinking, what she wants, that will get her farther with the men in the rest of her life than platinum curls or a 36-23-36 figure. She will learn to ask, "May I come along?" instead of grieving silently because her father didn't suggest it. She will learn to say, "Dad, for my birthday next month I know exactly what I'd love to have," instead of growing into one of those martyred women who use forgotten anniversaries as a sword above their husbands' heads.

Learning that men and women react differently to the same stimulus will be an important part of your daughter's growing up. There's so much advice about parents agreeing on child-raising matters that we've become frightened of differences. Of course it confuses a child when she finds herself the center of conflict. But differences need not mean conflicts; in fact, conflict over raising their child usually reflects tensions in other areas of a couple's relationship and has little to do with the actual situation they are fighting about.

If love is there, children will not be harmed by different standards and opinions. In fact, the little girl whose mother approves of her unreservedly regardless of what she says or does is lucky, but she is twice as fortunate if she has the balancing effect of a father who sees her more critically, demanding her highest efforts, challenging her by his own high standards. Or vice versa. If one parent is quiet, withdrawn, the other a gregarious soul, that simply makes for a well-rounded daughter who understands both types of people. *If* love is there. *If* the parents themselves have no bitterness because of their differences.

Even though a father and mother attend the same church, two people seldom are in complete agreement about all their religious and philosophical beliefs. But they can still be in harmony about them. And if they are, their child can be twice as rich in knowledge and wisdom because she sees the world from two viewpoints.

The elderly pediatrician who cared for Lindy when she was tiny used to say that at any age a child is smarter than her parents give her credit for being. After ten years and three girls I'm just about convinced.

It used to bother me that my husband wasn't more enthusiastic when he praised the girls for a job well done. I'd make a big fuss about a drawing or a report card, but he would study it in silence, then comment quietly, "That's much better," or "Very good," and hand it back. But I have found that the girls make their own mental adjustments, allowing for our differences, and they will glow over a very slight word of praise from him while taking my enthusiasm for granted. Since probably neither of us could change our basic personalities, it's fortunate that children are such flexible little animals.

Dr. David Goodman, who writes the syndicated column, "What's Best for Your Child," made a statement every worried mother should paste on the mirror above the kitchen sink where she will read it three times a day:

A wife who finds that her husband is at odds with her on how to bring up their child would do well to look to her marital defenses. A happy husband would not behave this way.

If he were very certain that he occupied the primary place in her affections, if he could have the satisfying assurance that his wife considered him the head of the household as she was its heart, he would feel a greater self-confidence in himself as a man and the more readily behave like one.

Women who contend with their husbands for the dominant position in the home win a barren victory. As individuals they triumph, but as women they are defeated for they have no man to be proud of, and they have provided their children with no proper father.

It's true, of course, but to a woman who has no adequate father for her girls Dr. Goodman and I must sound unbearably smug. On our local television station we have a husband-and-wife team whose shows lean heavily to the preparation of exotic gourmet foods. One week they devoted a program to making do with odds and ends when unexpected guests dropped in, and it turned out to be a program that has become a family joke.

First they took several cans of shrimp from the pantry shelf, next, a roast chicken was removed from the freezer and thawed, then the refrigerator yielded a pint of whipping cream, etc. Now, though several years have passed, whenever we hear a giver of advice who has no realistic idea of the problems involved, one of us is bound to say, "First take three cans of shrimp." That's just about the situation here.

I'll admit I've had to cope with none of the behavior that can break a wife's—and a daughter's—heart. But I've been close to plenty of women who have; close enough to know that just loving some men certainly isn't enough to transform them into adequate fathers. "Women who contend with their husbands for the dominant position in the home," says Dr. Goodman, "win a barren victory." But what of the mother who has to step in and assume the dominant position because her husband is too immature or too disinterested to assume it himself?

From women who have faced that situation I have garnered three suggestions:

HELP   ACCEPTANCE   COMPENSATION

These were not offered as three separate steps, but as one continuing program. Help may mean as simple a move as talking things over with your clergyman or doctor (*not* your neighbor or your mother!). But too many women shy away from professional help if it requires anything more involved than that. Yet I've heard mothers say, "My child's life could have been so different if I had only known how much help was available."

As a first step, call the Family Service Agency (they're in the phone book) in your own city or the city nearest you. Make an appointment *and keep it*. Don't listen to the little voice that will whisper in your ear on the appointed day.

They may not be able to help you change your husband (that's what most women expect when they seek counseling—help in changing their husbands), but if they can't, they will help you learn how to make the best of a bad situation. If you can do that, if you can learn to say, as in other times of crisis, "That's the way of it," and go on from there, you will be ready to help your daughter develop the same healing acceptance.

If your husband is an unsatisfactory father because of a drinking problem, did you know that one of the many services Alcoholics Anonymous perform is for the children of an alcoholic who refuses help? Often they are able to guide the children to a deeper understanding of their father's needs and weaknesses and despair. Call or write the A. A. chapter in your city and ask about Alanon.

Seeking help is always worth the effort, whether it transforms your home life overnight or just helps a little. Perhaps it's because I lost my own father through divorce that I feel so strongly, but I'm convinced that almost any father (a dope addict or one who beats the children or you is the only exception I'd make) is better than no father at all, particularly if the situation is skillfully improved by an intelligent and resourceful mother.

Which brings up the matter of compensation. If a father fails to be a father, the first step, of course, is to find father substitutes to take over many of the father functions. The line of least resistance is to take over the family yourself. But Dr. Paul Popenoe, of the American Institute of Family Relations, offers some jolting figures on where that line of least resistance leads. A husband-dominated home is 50 per cent more likely to be happy than a home dominated by the wife, while a fifty-fifty partnership works out to be 100 per cent happier than a home dominated by the wife. The answer is not, obviously, for us to be imitation fathers. The answer is to be absolutely superb mothers! And when a woman handles her own feminine job superlatively, it's reassuring to see how her husband's inadequacies become much less conspicuous.

If you are a divorcee, you may find that your former husband will be a far more satisfactory father on this new part-time basis than he ever was before, if you are big enough to allow it. Dr. Spock wrote an excellent article on how to utilize these part-time fathers in the *Ladies' Home Journal* for September 1958.

Recently I read of a little girl who lost an adored father through divorce. He lived three thousand miles away, and found it impossible to visit her often. The greatest source of sorrow to the youngster arose because of her playmates; her father, whom they had never seen, was so shadowy a figure that they scarcely believed he existed. Then her mother hit upon the idea of a bulletin board in her child's room, where the father's picture, his latest letters, and souvenirs of their vacations together could be displayed. The problem eased at once, thanks to this understanding mother who put her daughter's need of a father above her own pride.

But whether you are divorced, widowed, or very much married to a less-than-satisfactory father for your daughter, she needs a live, close, adult male influence in her young life.

Better yet, she needs several, so that she scatters her affection and dependency rather than focusing all her longing for a father on one poor bewildered uncle or friend who is bound to fail her just because he isn't her father. Family friends, uncles (if she's very, very lucky you may find her an uncle like the Uncle Thornton of my childhood, who will initiate her into the outdoor miracles of stars and birds and plants), grandfathers, even neighbors, are excellent prospects for filling the gap. So are suitors, if you're free.

And the very best father substitute, not really a substitute at all, is a loving stepfather.

Don't overlook the role of your child's playmates' fathers in her life. If you are willing to carry a little more than half the load in entertaining, feeding, and just plain welcoming other little girls, you'll find you can arrange a great many chances for your child to visit them and bask in the vicarious pleasure of having a real father.

Fortunately such extremes are few and far between. Most of us have a lot to work with in the way of ingredients for a happy family. But wives of even the best of fathers need to check ourselves now and then to make sure we're giving them the backing they deserve.

Even when Dad is at the office, we can be shaping our little girls' mental picture of him. By our own attitudes, by the way we talk about him, we are either tearing him down or building him up in their eyes. When you hear a mother saying: "We'll see what Daddy thinks," or "Daddy can probably fix it as good as new," or "Run and show your father how pretty you look," you can feel Dad being elevated to the head of the family. When you see a home where the father signs all report cards, says grace, and carves the roast, you know you're in a home where Dad is up there where he belongs.

And when you see a father who's the real head of the family you can be pretty sure it's because a sensible, farsighted mother planned it that way!

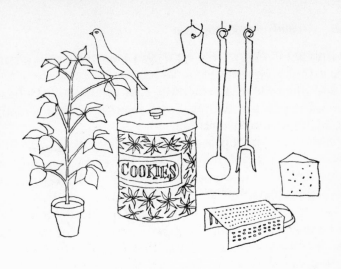

CHAPTER 7

Home Is for the Children, but . . .

Now that we've learned our lesson about hospitality I wish I could scrawl in big, black crayon letters across the walls of every dining room in the country: *HOME IS FOR THE FAMILY.* Does that sound selfish? Yes, I suppose it does. But like every bald statement it requires interpretation.

There was a time, and quite a gay and delightful period it seemed at first, when our home was the full-time social center of the grade-school set. By four o'clock on school days—or as early as their mothers could get them dressed and out from underfoot on other days—our walls began to rock and shudder under the impact of our children's friends. We were famous for blocks around for a bottomless cookie jar and a free hand with the Band-Aids.

Our children played at our house, their friends played at our house, and their friends' friends played at our house. Wherever we lived, there was always one child who came in time for breakfast and another who said, "My mother says I can stay for supper if you ask me." Or sometimes both situations wrapped up in the same child.

"Oh, well," my husband and I would reassure each other, "home is for the children, after all." We were wrong, of course; home isn't for the children. But we hadn't learned that yet. And how wonderful it seemed for the children to have a home where their friends were always welcome. Having missed that privilege in our own childhood, we valued it all the more dearly for our three. Here at last was that friendly home of which we'd dreamed since we first met, holding out its welcoming arms to our children and their friends, with promises of love and warmth and laughter.

Except that it wasn't working out that way.

Somehow that welcome mat was getting in the way of the love and warmth and laughter. It was bad enough when the children were toddlers. But as they grew, they developed into people, fascinating, provocative, nice little people. I wanted, not unreasonably, surely, to get to know them better, to have some of those happy family hours I had always thought were the reasons for families. But we couldn't. On walks, picnics, shopping trips, around the lunch table, or just quiet evenings by the fire, we were never alone together. The house was always untidy; Laurie and Lindy seemed forever at each other's throats (each with her own loyal, pugnacious following); Joyce, the baby, robbed of her afternoon nap by noise and overtaxed by excitement and confusion, was cranky and snappish by the time Daddy got home. And more and more often, evening found me pretty cranky and snappish myself.

Besides, there were never enough cookies left for dessert. That's what finally made me explode. The cookies. One morning I came back into our supposedly empty kitchen to find a neighbor's daughter raiding the cookie jar. I can't remember, mercifully, no doubt, all that I said, but it began with a loud, firm "Get your hand out of that cookie jar!" and ended with the youngster hightailing it down the back stairs.

For quite some time after that the girls weren't allowed any company.

And that was pleasant, too, at first. Little Joyce waxed plump and placid, the house was always (well, almost always) neat, and Laurie and Lindy were practically never at home. "This is more like it," I told myself, now that we could sit quietly, my husband and I, and read the evening paper in relative peace. "Home should really be for the parents." But this was all wrong, too, of course, and deep inside I knew it. This wasn't our idea of a home either.

Well, then, what did I want? More important, what did the whole family want?

We gave that a lot of thought and quite a bit of prayer. We even scheduled an entire Family Council meeting around that one question, holding a sort of brainstorming session, to get the girls' viewpoints and to clarify our own.

And now everything's beginning to work out all right.

Everything is all right just because we changed our emphasis. We talked a great deal that evening, but we didn't come up with long lists of rules, or complicated schedules for visiting, or for limiting the number of guests—we just adopted a whole new outlook: *HOME IS FOR THE FAMILY.* And if you are limping along with either a child-centered or a parent-centered home, try a family-centered home and see the difference.

Besides that vital basic premise, some very good ideas grew out of that meeting; it's humbling sometimes to see just how good the results can be when children's minds are given free rein.

First of all, they agreed we would have no more wandering in and out. Every child who came in to play must be the invited guest of one of our daughters. And each daughter would be responsible for the behavior of her own guests. In practice, it has been a very smooth operation, relieving me of fruitless nagging and creating, instead, a situation where they police each other. They've developed greater respect for the values of cooperation, inviting most often the children they know will carry their own weight, whether in cleaning up or quieting down, and playing *outside* with the ones who frequently get them into trouble in the house.

You can see how well the invitation system works. Did Susie write her name in tooth paste on the dresser yesterday? Then today the word goes out from me that Susie is *persona non grata* at our house for a week, or for a month if it was the good blond mahogany dresser. And if one daughter didn't see to it that her gang put away the contents of the game chest yesterday, she can't have any guests today.

The most drastic change we made in our family life was that now some children are permanently excluded from invitations.

That was a decision we made with the full knowledge of just how serious a step we were taking. But every family has a personality, a family feeling. Friends who reinforce and enhance this atmosphere are welcome; those who undermine and clash with it are a threat to the family and are kept out.

Not that we want for friends only those who think as we do —nothing could be more dull. And surely the greatest disservice we can do a daughter is to limit her friendships to children we consider "good enough" for her. Every child needs two kinds of friends, some to look up to, others whose values are on a different plane. But there are people, and surprisingly often they are children, whose presence rips across the fabric of a specific family, or any family, and allows the vital essence to drain away.

No such thing as a bad child? Perhaps not, in theory. But in practice there are children, or more often combinations of children, who are bad for a specific family.

Yes, I know. With so many disturbed, unhappy, unloved

children on every hand how can we bear to turn our backs on them?

We mustn't, of course, except as a last resort. The transformation the love of a good neighbor can work on an unhappy child is very nearly a miracle; the number of lives changed forever because a miserable, misunderstood child was gathered in by someone else's warmhearted, understanding mother are beyond reckoning. But these are not the children I mean.

No, I mean the rare child who doesn't respond to our love, or to any other approach we try—the bully, or the sneaky one, or the seriously disturbed child. It has been my experience that unless we are prepared to take such a child into our own home, raise her as our own in every way, we cannot do any lasting good. Oh, it can make us feel righteous; the role of Lady Bountiful, dispensing gracious understanding with a lavish hand, is a tempting one. But we are mothers, not social workers, not child psychologists. We may soothe, we may comfort, temporarily, but as long as the child returns at night to the same home from which she came we cannot transform her on a few-hours-a-day basis. And in trying to mother the whole neighborhood, it is fatally easy to fail as a mother to our own.

No, I've had enough of the children who rifle our dresser drawers, read our mail, swing Tarzan-like from the draperies, and stuff the towels in the toilet. I'm convinced that the only answer is to harden our hearts with a good brace of common sense and close our doors against them until such time as they can convince us they have changed. To be fair, to really consider the good of the family, we should go a step further and eliminate just as ruthlessly any adult friends whose influence on the whole family is disruptive.

I'll admit I had more than a few qualms about this strict new regime. Would I be able to enforce it? What if a visiting child simply defied me? But so far, instead of resenting our strictness, the children seem to lean on it. From the yard next door I heard a child exclaim, snatching up her doll clothes and paraphernalia, "All right, then, we'll just go to Laurie's house to play; you won't get away with that over there!"

The nice, safe thing about disciplining the neighbors' offspring is that you are nearly never challenged. The child won't tell his mother, because he doesn't want her to know he was out of line. And the mother, if she does get wind of something, is more apt to close her eyes discreetly than to make an issue. I'm speaking now of non-physical discipline, let me warn you. Spanking, when applied to another family's child's bottom is tactless, dangerous, and illegal. But as our daughters grow older we must all face our willingness or reluctance to go to extremes when faced with an extreme situation.

I read last week of a home in a nice section of our city where crashers invaded a teenage party and wrecked furniture, poured soft drinks on the rug, and shattered dishes, while the horrified parents looked on helplessly. Now that's perfectly ridiculous! There are times when being a battle-ax—calling the police, perhaps, or even wielding a well-aimed broom—would be justified. When her family is threatened, no woman can afford the luxury of helplessness.

But fortunately such dramatic encounters are few at any age. Usually all it takes to restore order at present is a sharp reminder directed up the attic stair well, "Lindy, if you're going to fight about it, you'll have to send Sam and Terry home." Of course the children have to know that you mean it, and that you'll carry out the threat, in order for the method to be effective.

Not that we send them home only when there has been trouble; sometimes we call a halt just to be alone.

Every family needs some time inviolate. We like our leisure free and undisturbed, therefore, no one brings guests into the house from dinnertime on, nor on Sundays. But I always try to be a good sport about help while I'm working. Doing yard work, or polishing silver, or cleaning out the garage, we usually have a convoy, but the children help make these jobs a lark.

You might do it differently—sharing your leisure but defending your workday. It's all a matter of what best suits the way your family wants to live.

Every family needs a place inviolate. No one plays in our living room now. No one. The living room is for quiet talk, for television, for curling up in the big chair with a book, for adults and for children who are in the mood to act like adults, but no one *plays* there. Your pet peeve may be having the children in the kitchen. Or you may prefer to designate the master bedroom as a haven from confusion and interruption. Just name a room and stick to it.

Ideally, this means providing another room somewhere in the house where there will be few restrictions; a rumpus room or playroom.

I don't know how I developed such a blind spot about playrooms, but I do know that in every place we've ever lived I've planned one spot especially for the girls—and the results have always been disappointing. In every case I got so carried away by my own plans that I lost sight of the basic purpose. It wasn't that the rooms didn't turn out attractively, but they just weren't playrooms. In fact, the restrictions against finger paints, coke bottle rings, and such defacing agents were even more strict in the new room than they had been when the girls had the run of the living room.

Finally, though, I'm beginning to learn my lesson—that the answer is simply less glamour. Whether toddlers or teens, children need a room where parental pressures are at a minimum.

When we moved into our present apartment, I had high hopes for the attic, a vast, old-fashioned one, dusty and unused except for the usual accumulation of the castoffs of generations. It seemed to offer an ideal place for the girls to let off steam on days too rainy or cold for outdoor play. But our youngsters raised a howl of protest.

"It's spooky up there," they wailed.

Finishing the attic was out of the question since this was rented property, so I had to put aside any dreams of paneling, carpeting, or even walls. Yet today, for a total outlay of $1.99, the girls have a colorful, much-beloved playroom, a playroom where for once they can really play.

We tackled the gloomy unpainted stair well first, sketching a big splashy tree, flowers, butterflies, and bigger-than-life-size birds. I'm no artist, and I used odds and ends of enamel left in discarded cans, yet the effect is quite as cheerful and whimsical as we could wish.

At the dormer end of the attic, posts and beams formed a sort of open room, with a funny little peaked ceiling. When we analyzed the various half-full paint cans contributed from the cellars of relatives and neighbors, we decided that the only solution was to paint the posts in alternating contrasting colors, which really adds as much gaiety as if we had done it from choice. The floor was painted in the shade of gray that results when six different brands of gray deck paint are combined, and it's easy to keep clean and leaves no splinters. (We never actually *said* that each girl who wanted to play there would have to go out and round up some paint.)

When all the bulky and noise-making toys were transferred to the new playroom, we discovered an unexpected dividend —the girls' bedrooms seemed far more spacious and uncluttered minus peg board, rocking horse, bowling set, etc.

By cutting up an old sheet, we achieved curtains at no cost, and then we finally broke down and made our one purchase: a light socket on a long extension cord, complete with a metal reflector shade. Hung directly above a comfortable old rocker we found in the attic, it makes a cozy, cheerful corner for the child who likes to go off by herself and read.

In the coldest weather light jackets (or old outworn bathrobes, which we keep on hooks up there) are enough wraps in our attic. But the best time of all is a rainy afternoon, with a spring wind slipping through the casement windows and the rain drumming on the roof. On such a magic afternoon the children insist that they wouldn't take the most elaborate rumpus room in trade for our $1.99 play corner.

I hope I've learned my lesson at last: that the dispositions of young and old benefit when girls and their guests have a playroom where playing is not taboo.

I hope the girls have also learned a lesson from this eventful year. Most of life's lessons must be learned the hard way, but surely a basic function of parenthood is to save our children trial-and-error bruises where we can. I believe that a little girl who grows up in a family-centered home will be spared, when she establishes her own home, the upsetting irritations of working out this balance for herself. She will have had years to build habits of organizing her time and her energies into the life that suits her whole family best. She will have had years of living by the precept that every member of the family has vital rights. She will have had years of absorbing that sensitivity to delicately balanced interrelationships that will make her able to fulfill the widely differing needs of her husband and her children.

Just before we adjourned that momentous family council I slipped this thought into the discussion and into the minutes: All mothers have an innate right to be inconsistent. That covers those days when I don't want a lot of children around, because I'm tired, or because Dad has a headache, or just because. The girls have the same right to occasional whims, we feel, and if Joyce has developed a hysterical fear of poor, gentle little Danny, we'll respect her right to be "safe" from him in her own home.

I eliminate any feelings of guilt by trying to balance this inconsistency in the opposite direction, by little unexpected treats for the whole crowd—a spur-of-the-moment tea party, a ride to the shopping plaza, pin curls and manicures for all heads and hands, or perhaps a cookie-making spree. This is an underhanded little trick to enhance my prestige with the children, and its works like a charm.

In fact the whole get-tough policy works like a charm—for the girls, for their parents, for the family. And now that HOME IS FOR THE FAMILY, we wouldn't go back to any other way.

There's an added dividend, too—now there are nearly always enough cookies for dessert!

CHAPTER 8

Take on Another Child

FROM a purely selfish standpoint you might look at it this way: if yours is an only child, you have to do it all for your own daughter—the lunches, the trips to the playground, the story hours, the bandaging of knees. While you're about it, why not do it for another woman's child and make it pay?

Then as you think more and more about taking on another child you begin to see that your own child will profit greatly from the project. Just as the too-chaotic household presents problems, so, too, does the only child's home. You know all the accusations—selfish, poorly adjusted to playmates, expects her own way in everything, too attached to parents—surely you've heard them all! You may even have asked yourself now and then, on a particularly trying day, whether there might be some truth to the legend. But you know, too, that there are valid advantages that only an only child enjoys. By taking on another child you can almost completely eliminate the disadvantages, so that your only child can eat her cake and—almost—have it, too!

But all this cool, deliberate calculation occurs only in the planning. Once you have actually taken another child into your home, you find that suddenly your heart's involved. What you gain soon seems unimportant matched against the priceless opportunity for service you discover. But that comes later, in the doing.

In the planning stage, giving day care to the child of a working mother seems only to offer a golden chance to salt away a tidy little sum of pin money—or winter-coat money, or finishing-the-attic money, if you prefer. The last time we did it —you don't have to be a one-child family for this, you see—was in order to buy a gym set for the back yard. Let's see, that was Mark. And before that, Gigi and Tad were for the two older girls' tonsillectomies, if I remember rightly, though those two became part of our lives for over a year, long past the time when the hospital bills were paid.

Another child offers a practically painless way to supplement the earnings of your hard-working spouse without disrupting your family life, without leaving your children, without even leaving your home. You simply, for six or eight hours a day, open your home and your heart to the child of another mother who is employed outside her home.

Easy money? Yes. But it's really starting your own business, and as in any business, there are pitfalls. We've had three children that worked out well, one that didn't work out at all, and in the process we've learned a few tricks of the trade that may save you grief.

In fact, I'll offer you a tested formula, though I admit it's not original.

Do something you do well.
Do it where it's needed.
Do it at a price that will attract buyers.
Do it at a profit.

This is the four-point formula set down by the New York State Department of Commerce as a guide to launching any home business. Let's look at this advice point by point.

Do something you do well. Well, I'm not sure I can go along with that all the way. True, if you detest child care, if the shrill treble of toddlers' voices set your teeth on edge, you might question the wisdom of taking on another shrill treble.

But it's an odd thing about this new business you're starting —it will make the care of your own child easier. The chatter, for instance; for the better part of the day your child will be talking to another child instead of to you; how does *that* sound?

You'll get more housework done instead of less, for you will unconsciously slip into a routine: indoor play, lunch, rest, snack, outdoor play. Suddenly many of the techniques of a nursery school become part of your planning. Clay and finger paints, such a mess to lay out and clean up for the short time they hold a lone child's interest, will provide hours of fun with two imaginations interacting. And for more than an hour of quiet play the trouble's small indeed.

The clever lunch ideas you see in the magazines—the clown-face salads, the cheese initials in the soup—all those are so much trouble when you've only one lunch to fix. But now every lunch becomes a party. The whole atmosphere of your home changes, and with the change child care becomes more fun for everyone.

If, on the other hand, you adore taking care of the small fry but resent every moment you spend with the vacuum and the mop, then this is surely for you. Here's the way to hire that cleaning woman you've longed for or to buy a washer-dryer or dishwasher. Then you can devote all day to the children!

Do it where it's needed. This brings up the problem of where to advertise. With two out of every five mothers of school-age children working, your problem is one of selection rather than search. Wherever you live, small town or great city, there are working mothers, and others who would go back to work if they knew about you. In fact, it may be best not to advertise at all.

Think carefully over all your near neighbors, the mothers of your own child's playmates. Isn't there one who's been saying she'd like to go back to work? Usually there is. If not, spread the word yourself—you've been thinking you might try day care for a working mother's child if you just knew someone who was interested. Give it a week. If your phone hasn't rung by then with an offer, branch out to a bulletin board. You're still staying close to home, you see, among people whom you know at least slightly, in an area where transportation won't be a problem. If you live in a large apartment development, a housing project, or a builder's development, you might post an ad on the bulletin in the office, or in the laundry room, or the activities building. Don't be too specific at this point about money and hours.

If your neighborhood has a weekly newsletter or shopping news, insert your offer there, not specifying too many details, but mentioning anything special you have to offer. If there's a park nearby, if you have a big, shady, well-equipped back yard, a wading pool, or if you've taught school, had nursing experience, or just plain have a way with children, feature that.

Why not the daily paper? Well, for one thing, you'll be drawing from a bigger hat, and the bigger the hat, the bigger the gamble. And if yours is a really big city, your ad will appeal to the drifter, the child who's been dragged from home to home, whenever an ad appeared for a closer one, or a cheaper one, or a pleasanter one. A child like that needs your help, as does her mother, sometimes desperately, but you may be taking on a bigger problem than you realize.

It's been five years since such a bewildered, belligerent little soul disrupted our home for four months; after five years there are still a few scars. I am not saying that you should hold out for a happy, well-adjusted child who will bring with her no problems, but I am urging you to take a frank look at your own family, your temperament, and your capabilities.

Are appearances important to you? Will you be able to give the same unstinted affection to a shabby, dirty, uncombed child as to a more attractive one? If not, be selective before you seal the bargain, not after.

Just how selective should you be? Well, there's age, first of all. An infant is perhaps the easiest age to care for, in some ways, but your own daughter won't have much to show for that arrangement. And it's a tremendous responsibility. We've found that a child just a little younger than our own, or halfway between, when we had two, is ideal. They're companionable, that way, but your child is likely to take a protective little-mother approach that gets everyone off on the right foot. Then, too, there's this—the stages the new child will go through you've already survived with your own; that will help you keep a sense of perspective.

But except for deciding what general age group you prefer, I'd caution you against too-rigid standards. Half the fun of taking on another child lies in the glimpse its offers of another way of life.

There was Mark, for instance, whom we took for one summer so that his mother could work to buy him school clothes that would look more American, and so that he could learn our ways and lose his accent before he started kindergarten. You see, Mark was British. My, but he was British! When he left us in September he hadn't changed a bit, except for developing an insatiable appetite for popsicles, but our daughters had absorbed his accent, his deep bow, his charming formality, and some of his impeccable manners. So don't be too selective or you'll exclude a lot of fun.

Then, too, it is axiomatic that the child who needs you most, whose whole life might be changed by your love, your children's companionship, and the warm welcome of your home, may not be an appealing child. To turn away from a lonely little misfit because she is not plump and pretty and cheerful may mean turning your back on the highest opportunity for service that life will ever offer.

Do it at a price that will attract buyers. If you have a blazing talent or a marketable skill, the going price for day care will seem laughable to you. But for most of us it's "found money." No carfare, no lunches, no career-girl wardrobes, and no more work than we have right now. Ten dollars a five-day week is the rate in our neighborhood at present, but the fee will vary with the state and with the state of the union. Run down the list of day-care ads other women have placed in the daily paper, calling each and asking her what she charges. That will give you a pretty good idea. But if you have something extra to offer, you may be able to ask a little more.

Here's one of the few extra-income projects where the rural wife is not at a disadvantage. The fresh air, fine food, and wholesome atmosphere farm life offers to vacationing city children are valuable assets, assets that working city mothers are quick to appreciate. If you are interested in taking on another child—or several—for all or part of the summer, contact Farm Vacations Inc., 500 Fifth Avenue, New York 36, New York, for information about listing your farm in their widely-distributed booklet, *Farm Vacations and Holidays.*

Do it at a profit. Ah, there's the rub. So many unforeseen leaks can drain away your profit and therefore dampen your pleasure in the work. Here are some of the pitfalls to avoid:

1. Hours. Set the hours to suit your husband's schedule, and be strict about the hours you've set. One extra half-hour can wreck your dinner hour, your husband's disposition, and

your family life, and your little paying guest, sensing your irritation, will be worried and uneasy.

Of course the hours may be made very short indeed. There's a great need in most neighborhoods for half-day care for kindergarteners, and after-school supervision, often amounting to only an hour or two, for older children. Your school principal may be able to set you on the trail of such a family. But of course the fee is proportionately smaller. And you'll need to look ahead and come to some agreement about school holidays and Christmas and summer vacations.

2. Goals. Save for something specific, and buy it *after* you've earned the money, not before. That's so you'll have an incentive to dangle ahead of yourself like a carrot. There will be days, never doubt it, when you'll be ready to chuck it all, but these are human lives you're involved with now; you can't just say, "Sorry, but I've had enough, thank you." The emotional security of the child you've taken in and even the livelihood of her mother are hanging upon your sense of responsibility.

3. How liable can you be? Your husband may want to check into the legal angles here, and talk with your insurance agent. We've always gone blithely along, trusting in Providence to protect our little paying guests, but admittedly it's not a businesslike arrangement. Keep an emergency chart beside the phone, with the mother's office telephone number (and find out how leniently her employer interprets "emergency calls"), her doctor's number, allergies to medicines and foods. If you plan to take your extra child along to the beach or picnics during the day, you will be wise to have her mother sign the same sort of permission slip your school or Sunday school uses. You'll also need a firm understanding about discipline—who's to administer it and how.

4. Do you need a license? Not in most states, but call the License Bureau at your city hall to be safe.

5. What about lunches? What does her child enjoy, what

is her attitude toward polishing off every drop and crumb? Just how elaborate are lunches expected to be? Will the child have breakfast before she arrives? If not, you'll have to adjust your fee; breakfast is an expensive meal. Are you to provide an afternoon snack?

6. What about "short weeks"? It's a real drain on your profits when the child is kept at home two or three days. You are still tied to your responsibility to be available, yet you'll make half your usual fee that week. Be as businesslike as a nursery school about it—they charge whether the child is present or not. In fact, it wouldn't be a bad idea to stop by a local nursery school and ask if you might have a copy of the form they use for such agreements and type up a similar one yourself. And while you're discussing agreements, what if *your* child is ill? Have you arranged to isolate her so that you can still care for the extra child, or will the child's mother lose a day's pay and perhaps even jeopardize her job? Now's the time to thresh these things out, not after you're in business.

7. Don't let laundry eat into your fee. If the extra child is apt to wet the bed during her nap, either have fresh linens brought each day or allow a little extra money for this extra chore. Be sure to have a complete change of clothes kept at your house in case of accidents or mud pies or spilled milk, as well as a jacket and a bathing suit for days that call for one or the other.

Set down in such detail the whole business sounds dreadfully complicated; it's not at all. It's truly easy money.

It's also a perfectly splendid way to provide your daughter with all the companionship a nursery school could offer. And have you priced nursery schools lately? Your own child will be happier, your housework will be easier, and don't underestimate this unexpected bonus—you'll know the warm glow of satisfaction that comes from holding out a helping hand to another human being.

CHAPTER 9

The Educated Heart

LITTLE children—be they boys or girls—are instinctively cruel, even savage. Everyone who deals with children comes to recognize this unpalatable fact. And you hear it talked about a great deal.

But little children—be they boys or girls—are also instinctively kind, intuitive, sensitive, warm hearted. It's a pity we don't hear more talk about that. It's a pity, because random kind instincts are not enough. It is only through guidance by a perceptive mother that a daughter gains the direction, aim, and techniques she needs to translate her kind instincts into action.

All through our country's early years charity was the concern of women—charity in its broad original sense of loving care. In some areas this meant ministering to a fever-racked woman in the slave quarters, in others, "taking to raise" a family of children left motherless in an Indian raid.

119

Today, despite our organized charitable agencies, charity is still the concern of women. It's women who carry the heaviest weight of long hours of volunteer work in hospitals and for the Red Cross. It's women who ring doorbells for fund drives, women who fill Goodwill bags, women who whip up support for foreign missions and for local hot-lunch programs. Nearly every one of the great national foundations for the aid of victims of specific diseases originally arose from the determination of one dedicated mother. Charity always will be the concern of women—charity in its fullest meaning.

So in a very real sense the future depends upon these women-to-be we are shaping, depends upon the greatness of their hearts and the facility which they can turn their kind instincts to the service of their loved ones, their neighbors, and the world. For kindness—if it is to be of real and lasting worth in a harsh world—must be directed, trained, and educated. It was Gelett Burgess who first used the phrase, "the educated heart," but it should be a part of every mother's vocabulary.

The gentleness, the deep concern for others which we all consider the mark of a womanly woman do not spring into full bloom at womanhood. The seeds of such "kindness with a flair" must be sown from the time of our daughters' first words, first gestures. The fragile plant must be nourished, cherished, and encouraged every day of their childhoods.

And never a day goes by that doesn't offer a chance for such encouragement, if we will only seize it. Is your grubby little angel banging on the screen door again with another fistful of dandelions for you? How old Mrs. Murray's face would light up at the sight of that offering! You have only to suggest it; your child's deep need to love and be loved will leap to meet the suggestion.

Is there a new baby in the neighborhood? Your child could ask the house-bound mother whether she needs anything from the store. A word of caution from you about doorbells and loud voices will make her gesture doubly welcome.

Or on a snowy day, when hardy youngsters will insist on being outdoors anyway, why not a food lift of sleds shuttling between the corner store and the homes of elderly or shut-in neighbors, carrying small but vital food orders? It's not just the snowy air that will bring a glow to the children's cheeks after such a mission. At any age it is good to know we are needed; for children, who are nearly always on the receiving end, being needed is a heart-lifting experience.

Now and then we hear the claim that our highly organized charity organizations have stifled the individual's chance to help his neighbors. Nonsense. Helping is helping, whether it involves going without candy to give the money to a street-corner Santa, or sending a dollar of precious birthday money to CARE, or handing too-small shoes to the Salvation Army truck driver. Our part is to be sure that our child understands why she is giving, to whom she is giving, how it is distributed (most such groups welcome visitors), and, above all, that her contribution is a vital one, no matter how small.

Unfortunately, charitable gifts treat only symptoms. Even a very young child can grasp the fact that to do any lasting good we must tackle the causes of poverty—disease, discrimination, greed, crime, lethargy. We will do well to impress upon our daughters their moral responsibility to tackle social problems on this deeper level wherever and whenever they are able, but meanwhile we can encourage them to treat the symptoms realistically.

Dr. Schweitzer has said that "our greatest mistake, as individuals, is that we walk through our life with closed eyes and do not notice our chances. As soon as we open our eyes and deliberately search we see many who need help, not in big things but in the littlest things. Wherever a man turns he can find someone who needs him."

At Thanksgiving do you invite at least one lonely soul to

share your feast? When from paste and scissors and paper lace emerge another year's crop of valentines, do you subtly plant the idea of mailing some to distant relatives, former teachers, elderly friends who are apt to be forgotten? Once you form the habit of encouraging the educated heart, you'll be amazed how many outlets appear.

The fine art of the compliment is a fertile field for cultivating the gentler side of our daughters. How many children do you know, or women, either, who can accept a compliment with a poised smile and a simple, unembarrassed "thank you"? Far more of us give compliments well than are able to receive them gracefully.

For that matter, more of us give help well than are able to receive it gracefully. It's not enough for our little girls to learn to give. The educated heart accepts help so gracefully that both she and the giver are richer for the exchange. I'm glad that we've always been lucky enough to have at least one friend or relative or neighbor with a child just enough bigger than one of ours to provide hand-me-downs. That way the girls have grown up in somewhat the same atmosphere that pervaded the early pioneer settlements: we'll help you today— tomorrow you'll be helping us. Such help carries no stigma, we want our children to know.

Help need not mean such tangibles as food and blankets and coins. Help, as the educated heart well knows, may be only a handclasp and a word of comfort. Help may be a letter of faith to a friend in trouble. Help may be remembering a birthday or it may be forgetting a *faux pas* or an old hurt. Help may be simply a sunny smile warming the heart of a passing stranger whose need of it may be greater than we can possibly know.

Entertaining is one of the very finest training grounds for such intangible service. Indeed, from the first time a little hostess learns to pass the plate to her doll first and to take the smallest clay "cookie" for herself, she is practicing the delicate art of putting others first. And it's an art that requires a great deal of practice.

Little girls especially love to entertain their aunts and grandmothers overnight, an event that can be topped off with the luxury of breakfast in bed brought in by your daughter. And more than half the fun is readying the perfumed soap, the carefully appointed bedside table, the laboriously printed breakfast menu. It's a very tall step toward the educated heart.

The role of guest is rich with possibilities, too. Just selecting the gift she'll take to Marianne's birthday party can point your daughter toward being a snob or being a gentlewoman. Do we make a hurried trip to the store alone, picking up anything that will do, complaining about the expense? Or do we fret about whether the $1.00 blouse is going to seem cheap compared to that expensive-looking purse our child received from Marianne? If we do, we are wasting a precious chance to help our child.

The nicest family I know gives real thought to the birthday presents they give. Pat and her little girl Susan sit down with pencil and paper and list anything the birthday child especially wants—hints she may have dropped, or toys she particularly enjoys at their house. If no clue appears, they explore the kind of child she is: feminine, tomboy, studious, artistic? Then Pat and Susan take their list and shop together, frankly trying to get the best value for their money, and they wrap the gift together, always with some bright, imaginative touch (they clip gift-wrap ideas from magazines all year long).

There is an aura of shy warmth about Susan when she comes to the party, proudly bearing her gift. The love, the caring that she offers her friend shines in her eyes and draws us all under her spell.

Christmas is a golden season for encouraging youngsters' hearts to grow. Then the very air throbs with loving and giving. At Christmas I always remember one thing that Philip Wylie said about mothers: "Be as unsentimental about it as you wish;

there is still no denying that the homemaker moves in the honorable tradition of the makers and molders of society. Here you are and here is the plastic clay, and when you have done with it what you will, here, after all, is the pivot center of the world."

Is there any memory we can build so precious as that of Christmas in a home where the children are a real part of the holiday; where homemade gifts and homemade decorations are cherished; where batch after batch of fragrant cookies are packed for the mailman, the milkman, the paper boy, the crossing guard; where hot cocoa and doughnuts are always waiting for the carolers on Christmas Eve? Such a home not only creates memories to cherish for a lifetime, it also creates children who, grown to adults, will found their own homes on the joy of giving.

Later, when Christmas or the birthday is past, another opportunity for heart training arrives in the guise of a problem—acknowledging the gifts. Long before she can write, a little girl can crayon a picture of each gift and mail it to the sender, a gesture guaranteed to gladden the hearts of relatives and to develop in the little writer a sensitive awareness of the feelings of others.

That's all the educated heart means, essentially—a heart that puts others first, a heart that cares about people, and feels for them and with them. Or, as the profound religious thinker and philosopher, Martin Buber, puts it so concretely, "Our goal is learning to love people and use things, instead of using people and loving things."

There are, however, three dangers involved in all this outgoing love—dangers so inevitable that it might be wise to stop and ask ourselves, "Do we really want our daughter to live by the ideals to which we give lip service?"

The first and most immediate danger is that she will take us at our words. If we have been teaching her that we must be courteous and gentle toward all people, she may come to believe that we mean *all* people. Are we ready for that? Are we ready to mean it, really mean it, without reservation or exception?

There are many who do. There are still many mothers who do not. But multitudes of us lie somewhere in between. We cry out with St. Augustine that we do not want to change, but that we want to want to! Perhaps we can be the bridge between the old way of life and the new, bequeathing to our daughters a philosophy of brotherhood that we cannot yet, quite, accept for ourselves.

Then there is the danger of starting out with wonderful intentions, only to be defeated by our own lethargy. There comes a day when we are too tired, too busy, too distracted with some desperate worry of our own to look outward toward our fellow men. That is something a child can understand once or twice or a dozen times. But if day after day she comes to us with a warmhearted, generous gesture that needs our help to be put into action, and day after day we dash cold water on her plans, eventually that warm glow of feeling will simply burn out. If we are to raise the kind of women we say we admire, we must pay the price of occasional inconvenience and sacrifice.

And third, when we encourage our children to feel, we must accept the fact that they will feel pain as well as joy. At some point an aware and sensitive child will come face to face with violence, poverty, cruelty, despair, and she will ache with the hurt of it. But such a child discovers this advantage: being able to do something about it eases the ache.

One winter day Lindy saw a letter in the morning paper, telling of a Korean war bride in our town, deserted by her husband, frightened, penniless, ill, with two little babies to support. The letter had been written by a neighbor of the woman, and she gave the address and ended with an appeal for help.

That was, I suppose, the first glimpse Lindy had had into a world where daddies don't come home for dinner, where little children huddle hungry and cold, and her reaction was so violent that it frightened us. But after her sobbing subsided and her tears were dry, we sorted through the cartons in the attic, collecting more than we really could afford to give. Then she went to several of the neighbors, showed them the letter, and triumphantly loaded the car with their contributions. Finally we drove to the address on the letter.

We found a tiny, fragile, infinitely charming woman and two beautiful golden babies. More important, we found that another family had arrived before us, and two more came while we were there. On the way back home Lindy seemed again happy and content; she had found that although there is tragedy, there are also many hands to help. I believe that she evolved a new strength from the day's events: the world might be harsh, but she, small as she was, could change it.

The growing number of service clubs among teenagers and pre-teens, and the wonderful response of older girls to appeals for nurses' aides, indicate that every age group craves the satisfaction of helping, the heartening knowledge that something can be done to ease the world's sorrows.

Don't be too quick to label that philosophy naïve. Don't be too quick to belittle the power of one educated heart. Just one such daughter can transform a home, a classroom, an office. If we produce enough of them, they can change the world.

CHAPTER 10

This Cold, Cruel World

THEY were building bonfires on the mountain the night our middle child was born; I watched them from the hospital window. Since late afternoon men had combed the pine forest, on foot and on horseback, looking, calling for a missing little girl. Now it was night, with the March wind blowing up bitter sharp and the mountain lions starting to prowl.

The lost child was such a little thing, only eighteen months old. While the men and boys tramped the woods, all over town women watched at windows, watched and prayed that fear of the fires would send the cougars slinking to the other side of the mountain. If she had simply wandered off, as we all hoped, then she had to be in the forest; if she were in the forest, the bloodhounds would find her. But it would be morning before the helicopter flew up from Phoenix with the dogs. Meanwhile, there were the night and the biting cold and the cougars.

For me there was irony in those fires on the mountain, because one reason we had moved to that small, high Western town was to keep our daughters safe. As with many city-bred people, the sordid dangers of our crowded cities had never seemed a personal threat until our first daughter was born. But with her birth, suddenly the trim green parks and pink magnolias and white marble buildings of Washington had seemed less important than the capital's miles of gray, rat-infested alley slums.

A year later, when we moved to a large Midwestern city, I felt the same oppressive sense of a jungle closing in. Finally, when the body of a small-time racketeer was found in a vacant lot just two blocks from our house, it was the final push. Not just the killing, though that was bad enough. But when the police announced that the beating had not really killed the man, that lying unconscious in the snow he had frozen to death, that therefore death was due to natural causes, and that there would be no police investigation, we were finally shocked enough to rebel.

We would get back to simple, elemental living. We would move to a wholesome, open land where children could grow up safe from slums, safe from rats and filth, safe from violence.

Yet here, too, in this peaceful place lurked danger, stalking a little girl who could easily have been our own.

Just before dawn a Ranger found her—scratched, cold, hungry, but safe—sleeping curled up against a fallen log. The incident was over.

But that night had altered all my old ideas about this cold, cruel world. We had simply traded man's inhumanity to man for the violence of nature. There has always been danger for our children; there always will be. Before the hydrogen bomb there was poison gas, and before that the Indian tomahawk, the crossbow, and the black plague. As a matter of fact, a pioneer mother, worked out and old at twenty-five, living in constant dread of Indian raids, watching the number of tiny graves in the orchard increase after each blistering summer, each nightmare winter, would surely see our time as a paradise of unbelievable ease and joy.

And most of the time modern mothers see it that way, too. We plan ahead for our daughters, confident that life will be for them substantially what it has been for us. Most of the time. But there come days—or, more often, nights—when the headlines panic us, when a black fear closes in, filling us with swift terror for our children, with a conviction that the safe, serene world we have known is dying.

Last night I stood by our littlest's bed, listening to the soft flutter of her breathing, watching the shadow of her eyelashes, the roundness of her cheek. Standing there, I was poignantly aware of all the mothers who must be lying sleepless on the hard boards of barracks in Soviet prison labor camps, staring into the darkness, wondering where their children are, even whether they are alive or dead. I remembered the item in last night's paper: an Algerian mother standing numb and speechless, rocking her baby in her arms as she heard a judge sentence her to twelve years at hard labor because rebel guns were hidden under her house. For a moment all the pain and terror and hunger in the world seemed to be milling outside our snug four walls. Somewhere right in this city a baby waked and cried because a rat scampered across her face; somewhere right in this city murder, rape, slashings, and beatings were making a nightmare of this night.

The mood didn't last, of course. Immediately I pushed such grim and sordid thoughts out of my mind. We all do that. It's not callousness, it's necessity. It's the only way we can preserve our sanity. To the extent that we can help, we do; where we can't, we push the jungle to the backs of our minds. We don't dwell on such fears.

Yet we must face the fact that the world holds more than our sunny street. It is no longer enough to raise our daughters to be ladies, polished, accomplished, refined. We must raise them to be strong as well.

That sun-suited little girl in your sandbox may marry an engineer or a boy who has to see army duty, and watch with her own sun-suited little one from a window in a far-off country where revolution is raging below them in the square. Even in the most familiar street in Suburbia she isn't truly safe. For what of the carefully reared daughter who grows through secure, uncomplicated years to womanhood, only to have death of a loved one, or chronic illness, or a crippling accident shatter her world? Then what? Will she crumple or stand tall?

That depends on how we've handled our dual responsibility: to protect her, yet to prepare her, too.

When it comes to danger our daughters have a tremendous advantage over past generations. There was a recent time when children in this country—especially daughters—led lives so sheltered that they needed to be warned that evil existed. Today's child, bombarded from all sides by spine-chilling newspaper and television accounts of horror, finds suspicion more natural than trust. More than warnings, our youngsters need to be shown that people are good, that the sight of a child warms them, and that when strangers speak, they nearly always do so from an impulse of love.

About this business of talking to strangers, J. Edgar Hoover has said that the vast majority of sex crimes against children are committed, not by a stranger, but by a person known to the child. Yet we condition every child (especially every little girl) from babyhood that every stranger harbors potential peril. The admonition is handed to her as she goes out the door, along with her fresh handkerchief. We so easily forget that "strangers are friends we haven't met yet."

Left to their own instincts, children's reactions may be

healthier than our own. Last December we made our annual pilgrimage to see the Christmas windows in the department stores downtown. We viewed them all, from the exclusive shops at the north end of Main, all gold and glitter, to the sleazy red cheesecloth and tinsel of Lower Main. Down there, when we were just about to turn back, an old man who had been leaning against a store front took one unsteady step toward us, smiling a nearly-toothless smile, and brushed his fingers hesitantly across our little Joyce's curls.

My reaction was to pull her toward me, a reaction of recoil which was probably understandable enough. But I'm glad Joyce's instincts were more civilized than mine; she smiled back at him as we passed and said softly, "Hello, man." Looking back, I wondered if those blue eyes and dusky curls perhaps lit a memory of another child in another red coat and bonnet in another world, another time. How much that old derelict must have needed her smile!

Of course little girls must be taught not to go away with strangers, not to get into anyone's car, but for friendly adults it's a chilling experience to smile and speak to a child in passing and be met with a look of cold and black distrust.

It's possible that I'm prejudiced about the dangers of speaking to strangers. I was a latchkey child, on my own for long hours while my mother worked, and more than once when I ignored the precept strangers led me through such delightful doors.

I remember my first ride alone on a train the summer I was six, feeling very, very adult with my lunch in a shoe box and my destination printed on a tag pinned to my coat. A salesman for a harmonica importer had the next seat, such a handsome man, with a continental accent and, perhaps because he had grandchildren my age, an understanding of the importance of being six and going to Aunt Gertie's all alone. When I changed trains at Wheeling he bought me a vanilla ice-cream soda at the soda fountain in the terminal. He held my chair, and ordered for me with courtly grace and gave me a tiny harmonica, no larger than a charm, that really could be played. Then he put me onto the right train and bowed and kissed my hand! Of course my mother was angry when I told her about it, and she was quite right, but what if I had missed that priceless memory?

Or what if I had missed the hot, dusty afternoon when time stood still while I played with the priceless collection of dolls at the Carnegie Museum, thanks to the good will of a stranger? They were stored in individual drawers, hundreds of them, arranged like the shelves of a library, reaching from ceiling to floor, with tall ladders that wheeled along a track to reach the highest drawers. I don't remember how it happened that I got myself asked into the office, but I remember, as though I were perched there now, the new-wax smell of the linoleum, the musty scent of the costumed dolls, the women who came into the office and paused to toss me a smile up there so near the ceiling.

Our oldest had an unpleasant experience with a stranger last summer—a drunk who drove slowly along the curb as she and a playmate walked to the drugstore, calling to them with phrases which, fortunately, they were too young to understand. But judgment is keener in a child used to meeting the world with open arms. From long experience with kind, well-meaning strangers, Lindy sensed the menace behind this man's smile with a sure instinct. They hurried on to the store and explained the situation to the druggist, who called the police and us, in that order. So now there's no more going to the store alone, no more trips to the fields beyond the highway for the first wild strawberries of the season, small and hard and so delicious. Prudent, yes, but it does seem a pity.

I've found that the freedom to strike up acquaintances is one of the joys of taking walks with our girls; all together we can talk to strangers more freely.

Once we had driven to Squaw Island to skip stones in the river, when Laurie (inspired, no doubt, by all that water) suddenly announced that we had to find a bathroom. We marched bravely up to the nearest house and found not only a bathroom, but a sweet old lady and a parakeet named Billy who sat on the girls' fingers and displayed his whole repertoire of tricks and vocabulary.

The Sunday I took Lindy to see a railroad station we were told we couldn't go beyond the gates without tickets. As we turned dejectedly away a porter who had heard the conversation stopped us and said, "You folks follow me and I'll show the little lady the trains, tickets or no tickets." He led us through a maze of echoing tile tunnels to the switching yard where coaches were being readied for their next trip. He showed us how steam was piped under the surface of the yard to heat the coaches. He lifted Lindy up into one of the trains where the whole cleaning crew interrupted their work to show a wide-eyed little girl the kitchen, the Pullmans. An adventure to treasure for years.

More recently the girls' first real pet was a gift from an elderly woman who lives near our supermarket. Months of chatting with them as we passed once a week convinced her that they were worthy of one of her kittens.

Everyone can recall a dozen such encounters, yet we recall a single ugly headline more vividly. That's unfortunate. We want our children to walk through life safely, yes, but don't we want them to walk gaily, head high, with joy in the journey?

For a son, the development of a strong, silent approach to the rest of the world may do little harm. But to foster in our daughters any attitude that would temper the sunniness of their smiles, or chill the warmth and graciousness that are the essence of their womanliness, would be a serious mistake.

If constant warnings are warping and nearly useless, what other weapons can we forge to protect our girls? A fine neighborhood will help. But vandalism and gang warfare sweep across the boundaries of "nice sections." Even if juvenile hoodlums were eliminated, the international hoodlums would still hold the threat of war over our daughters' clean, calm world. If crime and war never touch them, illness or a crippling accident, or the death of someone dear can turn their sunny lives into a nightmare without warning. We realize, when we dare to face facts, that our protective barriers are frighteningly easy to scale. And though we cannot keep from our girls forever the fact that life can be cruel, we cheat them if we let the harshness of life eclipse its beauty. When Felix Salten created Perri, he gave our family a phrase that has helped us through countless times of real and imagined crisis: *It's a lovely world, but not an easy one.*

We've had pages and pages about the lovely side of life throughout this book; now, how can we prepare our children for life's other face? How can we prepare our girls for danger and pain and grief?

I've had a disgracefully happy life, so in planning this chapter I turned to women who have suffered. I put the question to them just that way: How can a mother prepare her daughter for danger and pain and grief?

The answer may surprise you. It certainly surprised me.

Every single response was the same—a happy, love-filled childhood, a rich cultural background; in short, what our grandmothers called a gentle upbringing.

That was a complete contradiction of what I had expected. Frankly, I was skeptical. But then I came across this similar statement by Vilhjalmur Stefansson, the Arctic explorer:

"Well-brought-up" young men are the best material for Polar explorers, or indeed for any type of "roughing it," except the sort to which the "poorly-brought-up" man is native. Generalizing still more: an educated man of diversified experience has the mental equipment to meet "hardship"; the ignorant are fitted to meet easily only those "hardships" that are native to them.

It began to make sense. If two women started out to climb a mountain, one after months of hunger, sleeplessness, cold, and privation, the other with every advantage of rest and top nutrition, most of us would consider that the second woman would triumph. Why wouldn't that apply to matters of the spirit, too?

Finally I consulted one last authoritative source: I phoned Gerda Klein. Those of you who have read her book *All but My Life*, who watched her, page by page, grow from child into woman behind the barbed wire of a brutal succession of Nazi labor camps, will surely agree that here is a mother who should know the answer to my question.

"Is it true?" I asked. "Did the refined, educated young women really fare better than the tougher girls in the camps and on the long marches?"

"Definitely," she answered, without a second's hesitation. "Definitely!" She was silent for a long moment, and then she said, "There are two weapons against disaster that the home can provide: the ability to think, and a background of beauty and faith to draw upon in time of stress."

I was glad, hearing those words, that so much of this book is devoted to the many faces of beauty. But what about the ability to think? We read in the evening paper that a party of young campers has been lost on a mountain, or swept over a dam, or trapped in a blizzard, and some perished and some, often only one, survived. Or a truck comes careening toward a car full of teenagers and in one split-second reflex the girl at the wheel saves seven lives. Why? What special steel had been built into that one young person?

How can we achieve this vital "survival training" for our own girls?

We can begin by being honest with them.

"Serious harm, I am afraid, has been wrought to our generation by fostering the idea that they would live secure in a permanent order of things." Helen Keller said that, and if we are looking for an opinion on meeting hardship, Helen Keller is surely the pinnacle of authority. She has more to say: "They have expected stability and find none within themselves or in their universe. Before it is too late they must learn and teach others that only by brave acceptance of change and all-time crisis ethics can they rise to the height of superlative responsibility."

When it comes to courage we tend to underestimate our daughters. In other parts of the world twelve- and thirteen-year-old girls are tending farms, rearing children (or tossing bombs beneath the treads of advancing tanks as they did in the Hungarian revolt). A fifteen-year-old Korean girl shepherded thirty little orphans, half of them younger than seven, through the war and somehow kept her pitiful band alive. Of course we hope to spare our daughters such an experience, yet the fact remains that women bear the brunt of family crises. These girls-who-will-be-mothers whom we are shaping need lessons in handling sorrow as surely as they need lessons in cooking or first aid.

Soon they will be women—women who must send sons off to war, watch husbands set out to do battle on the economic front under breaking-point pressures, deal with the many-sided fears of their own children. It is women who must mobilize the strength of the family to meet economic calamities, uprooting moves to far communities and sudden illness and accident.

To her husband and her children she will be the symbol of security. In a crisis someone must give them the conviction that everything is going to be all right. Since time began Mother has been that someone. As long as her voice is steady and her head is high, nothing can shatter her family's belief in the future. But how do we produce daughters with the strength to rally, rather than reel, in the face of disaster?

We can face with them, from their earliest years, the bittersweet nature of life, not as a complaint, but as a challenge.

When we pretend that life is a cotton-candy dream, we

don't fool our youngsters. In every age, and most of all in ours, childhood has its times of black shadows and nameless, paralyzing fears. When we deny the dangers they sense, we leave them so dreadfully, nakedly alone. That's the real terror of a child's world—being shut away alone with her fears. If she can speak of her fears to us, then she is no longer alone.

When the United States dispatched the Marines to Lebanon, there was war talk in the papers, on the television channels, in the very air. Like most parents, we tried to pooh-pooh the possibility, but that only made Lindy more anxious. A neighbor suggested the opposite approach, which had worked wonders for her family. So we stocked canned goods and blankets in the corner of the basement we had agreed was the best for shelter. We made a list of first-aid supplies we needed, and took the girls along to shop for them. We said, in effect, "There isn't one chance in a million war will come, but if it should, here is what we would do...." And our neighbor was right: it worked. That same principle—facing facts, then mapping a course of action—can be carried over into other areas of fear.

You might try calm, unemotional fire drills every few months, to reassure the child who wakes in the night sure that she smells smoke.

Some mothers, as soon as they move to a new neighborhood, spend the weekends taking long, exploratory family walks, spotting landmarks, eliminating the chance of the children getting lost. As soon as a little girl can talk she should be taught to tell her name and her address when she's asked. "You're never really lost if you know where you live," is one of our comforting family clichés. It is important that all children know the value of the telephone in an emergency, know how to dial the operator and ask for help.

If every daughter old enough to drive a car were drilled in the proper procedure in case of accident, fewer young people would panic and leave the scene. Your insurance company will send you a sheet on the recommended procedure.

When a child is old enough to talk, she's old enough to be taught what to do if she's lost in a store. Later you can introduce her to that useful feminine insurance—mad money. Lindy, who's ten now, and old enough to wander pretty far afield, wears a dime tucked into the instep strap of each loafer so that she has phone money and bus fare no matter where she is.

There is a supreme confidence about a child who knows what to do. I've seen children near hysteria because they came home to find the door locked and their mother late getting home from marketing, while another child will calmly follow the procedure her family has outlined for that possibility.

Scouting, with its emphasis on self-reliance and its training in specific survival techniques, can be a valuable ally in this project of making our daughters strong.

So, too, can stories of what other children have done. Psychologists have found that children are fascinated by tales of the achievement of other youngsters against terrible odds. Haven't the all-time favorite stories of childhood always been tales of daring and danger with a liberal lacing of tragedy and tears?

Equally inspiring are family legends of heroism. Grandparents who insist on recounting harrowing tales of battles, pogroms, or epidemics can be a problem, yet there is this to be said for their oratory, they instill in a child the faith that though life is perilous, man survives, that we can meet danger and conquer it.

But when someone dear to your child meets danger and fails to conquer it, what then? How you handle a death in the family depends on your own faith, on your child as you alone know her, and on the degree of your own emotional involvement. In short, there are as many right ways to help a child come to grips with loss as there are children. Child psychologists are maddeningly noncommittal on the many questions that confront a mother in such a crisis. But perhaps they are wise—most such decisions cannot be made by strangers. So much depends upon the family pattern and upon local customs or the nationality background of the family group. In many neighborhoods it is assumed that a child will attend the funeral of even a distant relative, will view the body and watch the casket lowered into the grave. In other circles such exposure to grief would be unthinkable.

However, I once read a theory I have never again seen mentioned but which seemed to me to make a great deal of sense. This psychologist insisted that the whole death ritual of our society was comforting to small children. He pointed out the often-observed reaction of small youngsters who have lost one parent or close relative and who later panic when anyone dear to them enters a hospital or leaves on a trip or is even late for dinner. This, the writer felt, was due to our tight-lipped "he's gone away for a while" explanation which make a child feel death is not far removed from her everyday life. But when the pageantry of a funeral is introduced, the child has something concrete to cling to. She can safely relax and feel that if she has not seen the long, slow line of cars, the trip to the cemetery again, then the baby sitter is telling the truth—Mommy really *has* just gone downtown to buy a pair of shoes.

I don't necessarily endorse the idea, I simply pass it along for what it may be worth. And there are several other facets of the problem that have been illuminated by the experts. We can be grateful that so much more is now understood about the reactions of children to death, for as women our responsibility is great. Just as the mother in our society is considered the citadel of the family's spiritual and religious life, so does she, in time of bereavement, set the attitude her children will absorb. A mother who can face the reality of death with calm, confident, fearless acceptance will be a bulwark to her bewildered children. Since these are mothers we are rearing now, the emotional security of their children and their children's children may well depend on how we meet our daughters' needs in such a crisis.

Of the three general reactions of a child to grief, the first is probably the one we've heard most about—guilt. It is not difficult to see that any child, looking back over a normal variety of gradations of love and hate, will remember times when she has fleetingly wished for the death of the person now dead. All we can do is bring her feelings into the open, explain that all of us have such emotions, reassure her that her thought had no connection with what happened.

The second reaction we should watch for is the disguise in which children often cloak their grief. A child may suddenly stop eating, or she may stuff herself neurotically. She may turn rude and sullen, or she may seem to ignore the whole experience and remain unmoved. In theory it should be easy for a loving, perceptive mother to spot the hidden anguish, but when we ourselves are heartbroken, nervously exhausted by the demands of our own grief, such behavior may strike us as grotesque and almost sacrilegious.

The third warning suggested by studies of children encountering death in the family is a valuable one, for it's apt to be overlooked by adults. That is the problem involved in the death of a very old person who was, perhaps, cantankerous and thoroughly unlovable. In such a case, not only is it unrealistic to expect our children to feel sadness or regret, but we may find that they are bewildered by our grief. We who can recall when the old person was young and kind and useful must somehow show our children that it is for that fine life we grieve. Also, if we will be honest, we can show them that even an adult's grief is often complicated by guilt over things done and left undone.

It is a complex problem, this first encounter of our child with death, and it is essentially a personal one. Yet when that child is a daughter, the problem is more than our own. The path we take may shape her attitude toward sorrow and toward death, seriously affecting her ability to deal wisely with her own children in a similar crisis in the years ahead.

Perhaps the only rule that emerges from the countless expert opinions on the subject (two excellent booklets are listed at the end of this book) is to be guided by what seems right and natural to you and to your child.

Of course not all a daughter's brushes with reality are so serious. But sooner or later every girl learns that bees sting, that kittens die, that neighbors come in loud, unfriendly models as well as pleasant ones, and that at least once in her school career she may be at the mercy of an unjust, embittered, or even neurotic teacher. The child who can say, "It is so," and then go on from there, has taken a giant step toward maturity and toward handling the same kind of problems in her own future family as well.

Mr. Disney, bless his understanding heart, helped our family a great deal when he cast Jiminy Cricket as a philosopher on the Mickey Mouse Club show, singing "That's the nature of things." Jiminy Cricket gave us the ultimate answer to the unanswerable. Is there a satiny butterfly trapped in a web on the hedge? Instead of tears, one girl will say to the other, sadly, "Well, that's the nature of things." It has been a deep well of comfort to them on many occasions, that calm philosophy of acceptance quoted so often that it has become a family motto.

I'm a great believer in mottos, clichés, truisms. One phrase the girls have come to live by is worth a half-hour lecture, we've discovered. "It's a lovely world, but not an easy one," a favorite I've already mentioned, is one the girls discovered on their own.

Another saying that we lean on heavily is one credited to the late Dean Briggs of Harvard: "Most of the work of the world is done by people who aren't feeling very well." Women need that philosophy. There is no sick leave for a mother. Although we may have been up all night with a feverish child, although we may be far from well ourselves, still we must keep going somehow. I've always hoped we could instill that brand of courage in our daughters, but for some years it appeared that our oldest was an incipient hypochondriac. The almost daily discussions as to whether or not she was well enough to go to school were unnerving for us all. But now that Dean Briggs's remark has become one of our "lines to live by," she takes pride in marching off like a brave little soldier.

That, of course, is the whole purpose of proverbs—to substitute a few words for many. And one of the most valuable examples is, "Sticks and stones may break my bones but names will never hurt me." Now we all know that names can hurt more than knives, but how many desperate youngsters have saved their pride with that old jingle, shouting defiance from behind the safety of it. And how many mothers have slipped the phrase into a trembling child's hand, like a shiny coin, when there was simply nothing else to give her. Quite often at such times the fewer words the better.

The first time one of ours came home in tears and confided, bewildered, that "Johnny says Jews can't be in his club," I launched into an impassioned defense of brotherhood. But I learned. I found that such epithets were usually hurled in a sudden spurt of anger, and that any handy name would do, just so it hurt—Fatty, Mick, crybaby. Then, in an hour, the quarrel forgotten, the children would all be together again. Too often, we read our own sensitivities into our children's experiences, charging them with too much emotion. So I stopped moralizing. Now I try to hold my tongue and just remind her about sticks and stones, give her a smile, a pat, a cookie. It's another case of saying, "It is so; now let us go on from there." I've come to believe that dramatizing such incidents simply sensitizes our children to future slights, and a child who is looking for insults will always find an ample supply. Soon the color of her skin or the origin of her name becomes a handy crutch to excuse all forms of failure! For a child who has lost an election or failed to make a club it's so much more comfortable to shout bigotry

than to face the fact that she may be dull, or loud, or untrust-
worthy.

Not that senseless, unreasoning prejudice doesn't exist, but
individuals from every scorned group have scaled the walls of
intolerance and made full lives for themselves, and our children can do it, too. On an impersonal plane we can fight prejudice. We can fight it with laws. We can fight it with example.
We can fight it by living lives so exemplary that at every place
we work, in every club we join, a few people change their
minds about whatever minority we belong to. Every one of us
represents a hated minority in some locality or in some situation—we are women drivers, or we are Republicans or Demo-
crats, or tourists, or we are poor, or, if we belong to the right
party, the right church, have a lovely home on the right side of
the tracks and skin of the preferred hue, we may be hated by
many just because of that good fortune. But fighting prejudice
is practical only when we are fighting for others. On a personal
level, if we are not to tear ourselves to pieces over every real
and imagined slight, we must learn to say, "This is how the
world is right now"—and go on from there.

Any child who is convinced that because of her ancestry the
cards are inexorably stacked against her might be handed a
copy of *The Importance of Feeling Inferior,* by Marie Beynon
Ray. It will come as a shock to a child who is wallowing in a
warm and comfortable trough of self-pity, and a shock may be
exactly what she needs.

Not that only mothers in minority groups are subject to such
tensions. In these days of shifting communities nearly all of us
have had some experience with in-groups and out-groups, and
our sons and daughters are nearly always sure to be the victims
of hurts they cannot comprehend, once they start playing with
other children.

But with little girls mothers have an advantage: remembering our own girlhood we can understand and help with a sure
instinct. The sweater she cannot have, the last-minute prom

date, the humiliating social blunder, these we can understand because they have all happened to us.

But not all the times of tears and torment come from without. Columnist Sydney Harris says, "The human animal has an almost infinite capacity to endure misfortunes that come from the outside—it is the blows we give ourselves, not those dealt by others, that really shatter us."

Of all the blows a daughter gives herself, remorse is the most shattering. It may be a transgression as serious as shoplifting, it may be a toddler's inconsolable grief because she has broken a lamp, or crushed a grasshopper. Whatever the crime, a sensitive child judges herself far more harshly than we would judge her. How can we help?

First, we can listen. Sounds simple? It's not. As soon as we learn of some reprehensible act most of us begin to talk. We rail, we cross-examine, we lecture; we throw a wall of words between our child and ourselves. If only we will listen, how much we can learn of the reasons behind the act. And oh, the comfort to the little miscreant to be able to pour it all out at last to an ear that listens and a heart that understands.

Years ago I learned from a very wise old woman a secret that's worth its weight in jewels in time of crisis.

"When something ugly, or harsh, or painful must be said," she always advised, "say it outside, under the stars or the bright blue sky, where the wind can blow the words away." Mysticism? I think not. Every sensitive person has had the experience of recriminations or painful words hanging in the air, making us hate the sight of a certain room or piece of furniture for a time. "Let's take a walk and you can tell me all about it," is a very good way to encourage a daughter to talk freely. Then, having thrashed out the problem and decided upon a course of action, home is waiting just the way you left it.

Having listened, we are ready for the second step. We can show her that she must face the consequences, but not alone. A child who must return a pilfered item to the five-and-ten, for instance, should not have to go alone. She must do the talking, but we should be there, warm and solid, at her elbow, condemning the action but not withdrawing our love.

That's the third key to helping our child through a bad time —to separate the action from the child. I've always remembered an incident that Ann Perrott Rose recounts in her book *Always Room for One More.* Just when they seemed to be making progress with a troubled, rebellious teenage foster daughter, Mrs. Rose found a highly objectionable book hidden in the girl's room. With her usual genius for getting through to children Mrs. Rose had a sudden inspiration while they were preparing dinner together. As the daughter stirred a bowl of gelatin, Mrs. Rose walked over and dumped the contents of the sink garbage strainer into the gelatin. Shocking, yes, but as she pointed out quietly, putting garbage into our mouths is not more ugly than putting garbage into our minds. That's the sort of objective, detached, but dramatic approach to wrong-doing that allows the child to stand off and look at her actions as separate from herself. It's so terribly important for children to know that no matter how much we hate what they may have done, nothing they could do will ever dim our love for them.

Earlier I mentioned that we once took on another child—or, rather, two—to help meet the hospital bills for the girls' tonsil-lectomies and that Tad and his sister became very dear to us. One morning when their mother dropped them off on her way to work, she told me that Tad was threatening to run away from home. His mother had told him to go right ahead and that she would even pack his suitcase. Our girls were still quite small, and this was a problem new to me. Tad went off to school, but I worried about him all morning. What if he really had run away? Finally I called the principal, who checked with Tad's teacher, who reported that he was safely seated in his classroom. But that wise educator didn't make me feel I was foolish to be concerned. In fact, he made sure that Tad knew I had called to check, and he warned me that a blithe, casual rejoinder to a child's threat to run away is the cruelest reaction we can show. Now that ours are older, we've heard the threat once or twice, and I've always remembered his advice.

"Please don't," I answer simply, as he suggested. "I would miss you so and worry about you every moment." No self-respecting would-be hobo can desert a mother who needs her as much as that!

The only other weapon we can give our children to see them through a period of sorrow, whether imposed from without or within, is a calm, deep, strong, religious faith. But of course I can't tell you how to go about that, for you can give God to your child only within the framework of your own heart's faith. Planted young and carefully tended, that faith will help to keep her strong through the worst that life can send. And our daughters will need all the strength they can get in the troubled years ahead. Then, if their generation is to see the destruction of the world we've known, they will walk tall and unafraid into the storm. If life brings ease and security, they will be the better equipped to savor them.

But "security is mostly a superstition." Helen Keller said that, too. Then she added a triumphant sentence, an inspiration for any mother who is helping a little girl grow toward womanhood.

"*Life*," says Helen Keller, "*is either a daring adventure or nothing.*"

CHAPTER 11

The Different Daughter

L ife is either a daring adventure or nothing."

It should surprise none of us that this exultant triumph over fear should arise from the silence and darkness that are the life of Helen Keller. None of us walks long through this world without discovering that the bedridden body often houses a wonderfully mobile soul, that in a twisted body the spirit often stands magnificently straight. Still, knowing this in theory does not ease the pain in our hearts when we are faced with the reality of a handicapped child of our own.

One out of every eight hundred new babies suffers from a congenital birth defect, in addition to the thousands of children maimed each year by accident and disease, yet for the parents of each of these the pain is as raw and incapacitating as though they were the first who had ever faced the tragedy. And when the handicapped child is a little girl, her parents face very special problems.

No matter how highly we may regard in theory the emancipation of women, our culture still stresses marriage and motherhood as the culmination of womanhood. For a woman, an attractive appearance and grace of movement are essential to the experiences that make up a whole and satisfying life. If a little girl grows up believing that her heavy steel braces, or her wasted arm, or her scarred cheek doom her to forego forever any hope of love and marriage, then we have really denied her the right to be a woman at all.

There is a man in our town who designs and builds mechanical gadgets to make life simpler and more complete for the handicapped. With wire and plastic and leather and chrome, he repairs twisted and maimed existences and makes them, not whole again, but workable, usable, livable. This man, who has worked with thousands of handicapped children and young people and their parents, has made a shocking statement. He was discussing the reluctance shown by many parents, especially by many fathers, toward opening the outside world to their "different" child. He was decrying the countless times he has watched handicapped daughters take their driving lessons and driving test surreptitiously because their fathers were violently opposed to the project.

He was, above all, lamenting the distrust and suspicion with which parents so often greet the news that a handicapped daughter has found the love every normal girl expects, and is planning to be married. Why this suspicion, this distrust? His answer is a jolting one.

"More parents than you would believe," he declares, "never really accept a handicapped girl as an attractive person in her own right. To put it bluntly, they simply can't believe that any decent man could really love her."

That is a dreadful accusation. And yet, no doubt there is more than a grain of truth in it. So often the handicapped child is a victim of a wasteful and tragic paradox: her parents

will give their lives and their savings and their dreams to make
her normal, but they won't let her *be* normal.

Yet, if it really is normality that we want for our daughter—
that is, a normal life as opposed to the miraculous disappear-
ance of her handicap—then the mothers of daughters perhaps
have a less tragic problem than the mothers of handicapped
sons. For in our cultural pattern, where the concept of the
clinging vine is still well entrenched, a woman's very weakness
may be her strength.

A *woman*—that, it seems to me, is the key word in rearing a
handicapped little girl successfully. Other children will grow
up almost by instinct; they will grow, molded and shaped by
the influence of the hundreds of lives that brush against theirs
in the course of their childhood, buffing and polishing them to
the final adult product. But the future of a handicapped child
—particularly the seriously handicapped girl—is in her mother's hands. Never for a moment must that mother lose sight of
the fact that this is a woman she is rearing, that these sheltered
young years are not all there is to life. Soon the child will be a
woman, and we want her to be a warm, outgoing, complete,
fulfilled woman. From her cradle days we must believe, and we
must somehow make her believe, that she is lovable, that there
is somewhere a man, a fine man, the true prince charming,
who will see her as we see her and love her as a woman needs
to be loved.

But how can we assure for her this shining future, since
surely to believe in the dream is not enough?

There are many concrete and positive steps that the mother
of a "different child" can take from the toddler days to adolescence to help make her daughter's dream come true. But before
we can take positive action, before we can act to change this
daughter's life, we must somehow find the strength that comes
with accepting what cannot be changed.

No one who has read Pearl Buck's story of her *Child Who
Never Grew* can forget the moment when the young doctor

stopped the parents in the hallway and told them to go home, to stop searching for an answer that they would never find.

Mrs. Buck says, "I remember that he looked cruel, but I know he was not. I know now that he suffered while he spoke. I shall forever be grateful to him, who cut the wound deep, but clean and quick." From the moment she made that decision she was freed, able to go on to the next task.

Such a decision inevitably involves heartbreak because any mother rebels against acceptance of a half-life for her child. It is easier to say, "No, we'll fight. We'll see one more doctor, one more clinic." Over the years the strength and finances of the family seep away, the lives of the other children are sacrificed, and for the handicapped child the vitality that should have gone into the positive work of building a new life is drained away to no purpose. Worse, she inevitably comes to feel that what she is is not enough; if it were, her mother wouldn't be so desperate about improving her.

Marilyn lives in Kansas City, in a big white house high on a hill. Marilyn's life has all the ingredients for triumph: parents who love her, enough money for the necessities and a few of the pleasant extras, a sweet, outgoing nature, and above all the most glorious young voice! For years Marilyn has dreamed of advanced voice training. Her teachers in public school believe she's concert-stage material. But Marilyn can't pursue her music because of her leg.

When she had polio as a toddler, only one leg was affected, but that leg hasn't kept pace with the growth of the other, and the muscles are atrophied to a point where the leg must be written off as useless. A dozen doctors have spelled that out to Marilyn's mother. But doctors can be wrong, she insists. So every afternoon Marilyn spends hours being massaged and exercised by her mother's patient hands, relaxing in the expensive whirlpool bath they installed when the doctors at the rehabilitation clinic flatly advised against further appointments. Summers flash by as they travel to one more clinic, one more treatment, one more man someone has recommended. There is no time for Marilyn's music, and no money left for advanced lessons. And Marilyn, who could be a fine singer with a pronounced limp, is, instead, a crippled girl with a lovely voice.

Yet it is true that doctors are sometimes wrong. Children who would never walk again become professional dancers or skaters. Then how is a mother to decide whether rebellion or acceptance is better?

I am tempted to answer, "Pray about it," but that is empty advice. If prayer has not been part of your life, you cannot turn it on now like a switch. And if prayer is part of your being, you haven't been waiting for anyone to suggest that you try it. Nevertheless, prayer is the first step toward acceptance; not frantic prayers for a reprieve from this blow, but quiet, listening prayers. The importance of acceptance (acceptance is such a meek and passive word, but there seems to be no better one) has been recognized by every wise mind from Plato's day to ours.

Jesus stressed it in the Sermon on the Mount.

William James said, "Be willing to have it so. Acceptance of what has happened is the first step to overcoming the consequences of any misfortune."

A modern writer, Agnes Sligh Turnbull, has included a chapter on "The Triumph of Acceptance" in her inspiring little volume *Out of My Heart*. Mrs. Turnbull has gathered together the thinking of some of the great minds of the ages on the heartbreak and joys of acceptance, and her book can be a great comfort to any parent who stands in desperate need of a little space of time "to stand from fear set free, to breathe and wait."

But there is also a fighting side to acceptance. Before you embark on any program to insure the benefits of a normal life for your handicapped child I would urge one final splurge on the best diagnosis and evaluation available.

Parents will go from doctor to doctor for years, spending thousands of dollars in dribs and drabs, when that same expenditure in one comprehensive visit to a top authority on their problem would give them their answer, in so far as human beings can ever know the answer.

A relatively new approach to diagnosis, and an approach that offers infinite promise, is the "comprehensive diagnostic center," ranging from the world-famous Children's Health Center of the Stanford University campus to four- or five-man teams of local specialists in children's hospitals in smaller cities.

This new approach to evaluating handicaps recognizes that a defect is not always simply what it seems. Such a broad program may bring together on one staff a skilled pediatrician, psychiatrist, orthopedic surgeon, hearing and speech experts, psychiatric social workers, and physical and occupational therapists. In short, this new approach to diagnosis measures the whole child, for physical and mental handicaps seldom appear singly. The blind or deaf daughter, in addition to her obvious handicaps, will usually encounter speech difficulties, for instance. And every child with a serious defect, congenital or acquired, faces stresses so much greater than other children that the worth of wise guidance counselors, aware of the emotional needs of each of these children and their families, is incalculable. Your own doctor will know the location of the nearest comprehensive diagnostic center, or you can get in touch with the well-baby clinic or visiting nurse association in your town, or write to the American Medical Association, 535 North Dearborn Street, Chicago, Illinois, for information.

In some cases the information comes to you without seeking, as in the case of blind children. In most states, when any hospital reports the birth of a child with a serious eye condition, a representative of the county association for the blind calls on the new mother and father, welcomes them into the Parents' Club, explains the facilities available to the new baby as she grows, provides comprehensive evaluation services, and in general makes sure that this new young life is started off on the right track.

In the final analysis, the number and the extent of the tests and examinations your child should undergo, and the age of which she is ready for them, must be decided by you and by your doctor, based on what you already know of her strengths and weaknesses and capabilities and needs.

Every step forward in the field of rehabilitation underscores the need for early diagnosis. A challenging new program now being carried on at the Hearing and Speech Center of New York City's Bellevue Hospital, as well as several hospitals in England and Europe, holds out the promise of "spontaneous speech" for even the seriously deaf child, but the success of the program is dependent on testing and diagnosis during infancy. The same urgency prevails in many bone conditions.

Yet every mother knows that there are children, especially very young children or children already emotionally upset, for whom a hospital experience can be a nightmare from which the child will not wholly wake for many years. A recent survey shows that children admitted to a hospital for diagnostic tests were being exposed to as many as fifty-two people in forty-eight hours. Because a young child's world is limited, she simply cannot absorb that many contacts with that many strangers.

Not only are there differences in emotional elasticity between children, but the same child's resilience will vary from month to month. Any upheaval in her life—the death of a close relative, the arrival of a new baby sister, anything that has shaken her little world—may mean that it would be better, all medical considerations permitting, for the hospital visit to be postponed.

On the other hand, hospitalization wisely handled can offer the very reassurance a different daughter craves, especially if she is one of a large family. The specialized attention, the extra care, the discipline of hospital routine, can be soothing if a child is thoroughly adjusted to the idea of being there. This will be particularly true if your child is fortunate enough to be placed in a hospital where procedures are especially planned for children and where enlightened methods have minimized the strangeness of her surroundings, and when parents have tried to prepare her for the experience.

If there are no such centers anywhere near you, you may find valuable information in *The Directory for Exceptional Children*, compiled by Eugene Nelson Hayes and published by Porter Sargent. This directory, first published in 1954 and frequently revised and brought up to date, lists schools, homes, services, and other facilities for children suffering a wide variety of handicaps.

The term "exceptional children" used in this broad sense is really an excellent one, far more so than "handicapped." For any child who stands out as an exception to the children all around her will suffer the pangs and problems of being a different child, whether her difference is technically a handicap or an advantage. The gifted child belongs in this chapter just as truly as does a little girl who is mentally retarded. This is particularly so in the case of little girls, who are born into a world where a woman with brains is still suspect.

The paradox of the daughter "handicapped" by a high I.Q. points up the very individual nature of all handicaps.

In our high school there was a girl named Serena, one of the teenagers who arrived each morning in the "Home for Crippled Children" bus. (Ours was the only high school in the city equipped with an elevator.) Serena made her way along the corridors by throwing the tips of her crutches forward, then dragging her legs and all their heavy hardware after them, then again the quick forward throw of the crutches and the long, slow pull.

Serena arrived at most of her classes late, flushed and perspiring. But never alone. She was easily the second or third most popular girl in class, with two or three boys paying court and a coterie of girls around her, too. Being the prettiest girl in the class helped, but it was more than that. She had a tremendous reservoir of vitality; since life was always exciting to her, it seemed exciting with her. At school dances there were three centers of activity: the dance floor, the punch table, and the lively handful of boys and girls sitting out a dance with Serena. Until we were seniors. That last autumn Serena's flawless skin succumbed to the scourge of the high-school set, acne. Within a time span of just a month or two her gaiety and vivacity drained away. She stopped going to dances, stopped laughing.

If a girl can rise above complete paralysis from the waist down, refuse to let it defeat her, then be destroyed by a skin condition, how can we classify handicaps as major or minor? A child has a major handicap if it is destroying her life, no matter how trivial the condition looks to an outsider. But there's a brighter side to that coin: a child has a minor handicap if she can rise above it, no matter how crushing an outsider would consider the odds against her.

And that, of course, is where she needs her mother. For after that first difficult step of accepting what cannot be changed, a strong, courageous, sensible mother can help her different daughter into the next phase of her growing up: minimizing the differences.

In many cases her handicap may be actually, literally, minimized. Such tremendous strides have been made in heart surgery, lung surgery, bone grafting, and neurosurgery that new hope is now offered to children who ten years ago would have been labeled "hopeless." New drugs have changed the outlook for diabetic, epileptic, and arthritic children. Corrections of harelip and cleft palate are now almost routine.

Far from being a tool of the aging actress, plastic surgery has become a vital force in the lives of many children. In fact, the American Society of Plastic and Reconstructive Surgery reports that three out of five requests for cosmetic surgery come from ordinary citizens.

Where the need for such work is immediate and pressing, few parents will fail to take advantage of the plastic surgeon's skill, but it is easy to underestimate the new confidence, often the whole new personality, that such operations hold in store for girls with seemingly minor handicaps. The correction of very prominent ears, for instance, is one of the simplest of these operations, and can be performed when a child is five or six. Rhinoplasty, or nose correction, undertaken ideally when a girl's nose cartilage has fully developed, at about sixteen, is the most common plastic surgery. A nose operation usually costs less than three hundred dollars, yet it can change a sensitive daughter's whole outlook on life. And the new technique of dermal abrasion has robbed acne scars of their terror. Frequently just the knowledge that her handicap can be corrected, that at some definite, specified time it will be corrected, is the finest kind of therapy.

Excellent booklets giving the latest information about a specific handicap are available from the Government Printing Office, the Public Affairs Committee, many insurance companies, and private foundations. Because the list is constantly changing, your librarian is the best source of information on pamphlets now in print.

This, then, is the hope that the world holds out to the mothers of different daughters: so miraculous are the leaps in our medical knowledge that yesterday's hopeless child is today's convalescent, and today's hopeless child may be helped tomorrow.

But you, her mother, cannot wait until tomorrow. Having found doctors to whom you can entrust the medical aspects of your daughter's problem, you are ready to take on the work which only you can do. The doctors may be able to make her body well, but only you can make her life whole.

Frequently the first positive step toward building a full and normal life for our different daughter is facing the question, "Where shall we live?" This is not surprising, for the birth of a handicapped child or the sudden crippling of a formerly well child has ramifications in every phase of family living. In every case the different child represents a heavy financial drain on the family income, which calls for a realistic reappraisal of our standard of living. Not only does housing represent an opportunity for specific cash savings, but the neighborhood in which we live, and all the subtle social pressures that characterize it, affect all other areas of spending. But finances are not the only factors that trigger a move.

The parents of an epileptic daughter must face the hard fact that in fourteen states their child will be denied the right to marry.

Also, help for the handicapped child still falls far below the need in many areas. There are not nearly enough special schools, workshops, rehabilitation centers, and evaluation centers. Those that are available are unequally distributed, with most located in the northeastern states and on the West Coast.

Consider the plight, for instance, of the emotionally troubled child; there are only about seven hundred and sixty child-guidance clinics in this country, and only about twenty-three hundred school psychologists. The same sad ratio of expert to patient applies in other fields. There may be no question of decision involved; it is frequently a simple matter of necessity for the family to pull up roots and move to a locality where facilities for the rehabilitation of the different child in their midst are available.

With many disabilities the opposite trend may be preferable. For the child with a very serious handicap, the small town or the quiet suburb where there is low turnover and a high percentage of neighbors who own their own homes; where, once accepted, she need not face over and over again the ordeal of the first meeting with new, strange children; this peaceful security of acceptance may compensate for the limited medical facilities.

Fortunately neighborhood acceptance becomes easier with every generation, as more and more of the old superstitions fall by the wayside. Yet in talking with the mothers of handicapped children I was told of two cases where families living with relatives were asked to move after the birth of a handicapped child.

It is not always possible to choose, but when you can choose the "character" of a neighborhood, most mothers have found that the neighbors in a section settled predominantly by young professional people—doubtless because they are the best informed—are the most tolerant, understanding, and helpful neighbors for the family with a different daughter.

But that brings us to a factor that must be faced in any attempt to help our daughters: curiosity. Whether evidenced by vulgar ogling and rude questions or by the politely averted gaze, curiosity is a fact of life for the different child and must be realistically reckoned with. About the curiosity of strangers little can be done. But the curiosity of neighbors, playmates, and new acquaintances is a different matter.

A courageous and resourceful mother, one who without rancor, can see her child through others' eyes, can turn this natural curiosity into a bridge between her child and the people she meets. One clever girl of our acquaintance, the mother of a cerebral palsied baby, prepared and mailed out a mimeographed newsletter to announce the birth to all her widely scattered family. Well aware of how little most of them knew of the condition, and equally aware of how many old wives' tales they had undoubtedly heard and believed, she outlined, briefly and factually, the doctors' findings on their daughter, and included a brief report of what little is known about the causes behind such cerebral injuries. A few were repelled. A few questioned the taste of her project. She had expected that. But most of her relatives and close friends replied that for the first time they felt they could congratulate and inquire and sympathize, naturally, without the embarrassment and constraint they had felt before. These family newsletters, announcing each new milestone, each new accomplishment, every new departure in treatment or training, have become a beloved family institution, drawing the different child into a circle of love and concern.

Embarrassment and uneasiness are attitudes that can isolate the different child if they are allowed to pyramid. Neighbors and acquaintances who don't know quite what to say will at first avoid the child, and eventually avoid the family. The answer is wonderfully simple and dreadfully difficult; the answer is simply to satisfy the curiosity. It is difficult because in order to talk casually and with a sense of humor about your daughter's handicap your own thinking must be remarkably straight. Parents' clubs of various organizations for handicapped children have grown at a heartening rate within the last few years largely because they fill this need on the part of parents to view their situation objectively. But no amount of outside help can substitute for the "willingness to have it so" which each mother must find within herself.

Last year there moved into our block a family with two children, one of them a little girl of four, born with only one arm. That very first day, while the neighborhood youngsters were still running up and down the ramp of the nearly-empty moving van, and eying the newcomers warily, the little girl's mother came out with a handful of cookies, motioned everyone to sit down on the front steps, and began conversationally, "I imagine some of you have noticed Debby's arm and wondered why it's made that way . . ." How much courage that took we can only imagine, but what wonderful results! Once their curiosity was out in the open the children asked questions eagerly and unself-consciously. Once their curiosity was satisfied, they turned to more important things—hopscotch and the cookies.

Whenever your small different daughter must enter a new situation, at home or at school, a few moments spent with the children who inhabit this new environment, explaining in simple terms geared to their age and understanding the nature of your daughter's differentness, explaining her capabilities and limitations, will often get your daughter started off on the right foot. Though never easy for any mother, many friends have told me that such sessions—provided they are handled with a sense of humor and a light touch, and especially when topped off with a holiday mood by the judicious offering of a cookie or a lollipop for all—can shorten by many weeks the period of adjustment of a small child to a new community.

An older child would resent such a step as unforgivable interference, but by then she will have developed, with your help, her own means of disposing of curiosity with dispatch. She will have learned that after that first brief moment of shock which most people experience when coming face to face with a serious, obvious handicap, the difference is immediately forgotten; you will have helped her develop ways to provide what one handicapped man so aptly terms "the moment of grace" for new friends. An excellent trick is the one many models and actresses use to ease the first nervous moment of an interview. This is the timeless, feminine gesture of slowly, finger by finger, and with great ceremony, removing her gloves. Any device will do, so long as it can absorb your daughter's complete attention for just long enough to give her new acquaintance that "moment of grace."

But curiosity and the problems that it breeds are the concern of us all, not just of the parents of the different child. It is one of the joys of being a mother—but it is one of the heartbreaks, too—that once we are the mother of any child we are the mother of all children. We cannot, no matter how we try to steel ourselves, look at any handicapped child without thinking, "There but for the grace of God goes mine."

Each of us has a responsibility to instill in our own children, no matter how happy and average and normal they may be, a proper attitude toward others' differences. This is not always easy. To make any headway at all we must think ourselves small again. Then it is not really too hard to understand the paralyzing fear very small children often exhibit toward any abnormality. It is a simple matter of self-preservation.

"After all," it seems to her, "if this dreadful thing has happened to that little girl, it can happen to me. I might even 'catch' it from her!"

If the mother of the handicapped child has explained her child's differentness in the terms we suggested earlier your job is easier. First you will get the fear out into the open.

"I imagine that when some children see Sally walking on her crutches, they must wonder if the same thing might happen to them. But all of you who have had polio shots are safe now." Or, "It is a very sad thing not to be able to see, but luckily the accident that made Bobby blind happened while he was being born, and only happens once in hundreds and hundreds of births." Once we have helped her face her fear, reassurances are in order. Such explanations should be simple and honest, but it is our own unspoken attitude of love and acceptance that will really reassure our child.

Fortunately it is this very identification with the handicapped child that will help her to be an understanding friend. We can help by relating the handicap to her own differences.

"Well, you know how you were born with that funny little toe that turns under? Well, just the same way Denise was born with that birthmark on her cheek. That's just the way she was made."

Or, "You remember how bored and restless you got when you had to rest your eyes when you had the measles and you couldn't read or watch television? Well, Sara feels like that, only worse. You see, all the pictures in the book look blurry to her and she can't see the programs on the television set, and even when she looks at you girls, your faces aren't clear to her, so is it any wonder that she has temper tantrums and gets angry so easily?"

If you haven't the information you need for this propaganda session, ask for it. The mother of the child you are explaining has drawers full of literature, and far from resenting your interest, she will be delighted and grateful for your direct, truth-seeking approach.

She also knows that the other child, armed with the facts, can be her ally in building a normal life for her child. For children look at things differently; to them broken-ness carries no stigma. To them the shabby Teddy bear who is losing his stuffing, the doll with no eyes and one arm missing, are as dear as the shiniest new toys under the Christmas tree. And so they feel about people.

How wonderful that this is so; for your different daughter needs other children.

She needs you as a mother, but you cheat her if you are also her only playmate. If you plan wisely, playing with your little girl can offer other children such advantages that her bed or her wheel chair or her room will become the social center for children of her age.

A record player, a large supply of games, an inside window garden, a full cookie jar—all will do much to widen your child's world. But for attracting small visitors nothing quite compares with pets. In a small city apartment a tank of tropical fish or a brightly colored and talkative parakeet or one of the fascinating, and escape-proof, new ant farms behind glass panels may be your solution. If you live in the suburbs, the sky and your local zoning laws are the limit, and the more unique the pet the greater its value for attracting young playmates. Rabbits, geese, a deodorized skunk, perhaps even a gentle burro—any one of these will boost your daughter's status and widen her world.

There are other ways to widen that world. The much-maligned television set is a godsend for a child who is bedridden or home confined. Here is the outside world brought to her living room, needing only your careful supervision to assure that the picture she gets of life from the screen is not a distorted one. Or you can encourage her to have pen pals (your librarian can provide addresses through which your child may get in touch with pen pals her own age), or perhaps the entire family can "adopt" a child in a foreign country. Though you, too, are confined to home you will not want to give up all contact with your clubs and organizations, and as your daughter grows, you two can work together on church and club projects —addressing envelopes, serving on phone committees.

Most important of all, regardless of her handicap, she can play a steadily growing role in the work of the family. A child confined to wheel chair and bed can do much of the cooking, set and clear the table, iron, and sew. All this requires careful planning of equipment, schedules, and layout, and simplified work methods. But the resulting sense of accomplishment, the sense of participation in the family as a working, contributing member, is well worth the effort and the planning. The American Foundation for the Blind, for instance, makes available special measuring spoons and measuring bottles for the little girl who wants to help around the kitchen. Many associations for the handicapped have made detailed studies on the equipment and techniques with which the handicapped homemaker can create a normal life. Several of these are listed at the end of this book.

In discussing chores, we stressed the sense of accomplishment that arises from a "specialty." Such a sense of pride is doubly important to the child who does few things well.

Mothers of daughters are especially fortunate in this connection, because the little specialties involved in homemaking can become, for her handicapped daughter, not only the basis of future homemaking skills, but also may hold the key to her employment future. For instance, the adolescent who likes to sew may find that a book such as *Sew and Make Money*, by Drucella Lowrie, will open a whole new world of possibilities to her, or will set her thinking about similar possibilities for being self-supporting. This business of being self-supporting looms tremendously large for the handicapped young adult, and it often makes the difference between a normal life and the captive half-life of an invalid.

The matter of being self-supporting can loom large for the mother of the handicapped child too. In America, at least, the working mother is here to stay. That the mother who is happier continuing her career than she would be as a full-time homemaker is also a better mother for the stimulation and fulfillment that she finds in her work is an accepted fact—unless the child she leaves behind each morning is different from other children. Because of this strange double standard, because of unrealistic sentimentality, even though the handicapped child may be left in the care of a nurse far more competent than the mother to handle the special needs of her little charge, still the Mrs. Grundy's weep and wring their hands. They cannot see that the working mother may return at night with a fresh objective viewpoint, with a renewed store of patience, with an outgoing love all the more abundant because it must be concentrated into the short evening hours.

But this is one more time where the mother of the different child must dare to be strong, must dare to do what seems best for the family as a whole.

In thinking in whole-family terms let's not forget that the handicapped child is spared many of the small annoyances of daily living—running errands, walking to school in all kinds of weather, the sometimes-frightening competition of other children her own age, often she is even spared punishment. In direct proportion as we spare her, we deny her a normal life. Even worse, we drive a wedge of misunderstanding between her brothers and sisters and herself.

For an adult, so stabbingly aware of all that this child will miss through life, the thought that her sister may jealously consider her favored seems incredible. Yet we must face the fact that in the things that matter so in childhood the handicapped youngster often has a very easy time of it. While her healthy sister goes off to school each morning, the handicapped child stays at home with Mother, sharing her day's activities, building a sense of closeness that only two people with such a close bond can possibly share, or so it seems to the healthy child. And for the normal child in the family there are always new dresses, new bicycles, exciting vacation trips that she must forego because of the constant financial drain that seems forever to haunt the family with a different child. The enforced quiet, the enforced patience, the enforced sweetness, the obvious inequality of time shared with her parents, all these may be interpreted as favoritism.

Where the situation has existed as long as the well child can remember, the adjustment is easier, but in cases where sudden accident, amputation, or very serious illness cause a sudden upheaval in the home; where overnight the family ceases to be a family and revolves only around the different child, the impact can be jolting on the other children. If, as so often happens, this dramatic crisis involves newspaper publicity, interviews, photos in the paper, bedside visits from local celebrities, and the resulting flow of cards of sympathy from strangers, it all seems crushingly unfair to the well child. This is where we can lean heavily on the principle of the educated heart.

Far from making her life miserable, having a handicapped sister can enrich a child's life. If she is sure of your love, if she never feels shut out, those very same extra demands and burdens that might embitter her will, instead, offer her the pride and sense of accomplishment that come of contributing to the family good out of all proportion to her age and size.

In the case of a brief and hopeless illness, or a sudden accident, it is only natural that the interests of all other members of the family must be subjugated to the needs of the different child temporarily. But when we speak of a handicap in terms of years, family life must be so organized that the mother can deal with all her children according to their needs, and still retain her identity as a wife and as a woman in her own right.

All mothers are entitled to chafe occasionally at the restrictions and aggravations and confinements of motherhood; but not the mother of a handicapped child. All mothers are entitled to days at the end of summer vacation when they sigh, "Three more weeks! How can I stand it?" But for the mother of a handicapped child even to think, "Ten more years! How can I stand it?" offends all that we revere as maternal.

Unfair though we know this attitude to be, the world does not change for individuals; but we can at least be honest and realistic with ourselves. We can realize our own fatigue, our own limitations, our own severe case of "cabin fever," and not be consumed by guilt, knowing that we have as much right to occasional complaints or isolated days of self-pity as the mother of any other child.

The mother of a child who requires more care than other children or of a child who is just around more than other children has as much right as any other mother to throw up her hands in despair. Indeed, in many ways she has more right than other mothers. Any sensible mother knows that she must pamper herself—for the sake of her family if for no more selfish reasons—during times when she is unusually tired, unusually busy, or under exceptional stress. Because the mother of a "different" child finds that this emergency state is chronic, strong measures are in order. She has the right to more time alone with her husband, time alone with each of her other children, above all, just time alone.

She has the right to extra help. This help may take the form of a part-time maid, or it may involve no more than the luxury of talking with someone who can understand her problems in a completely objective light. Psychiatric counselors and guidance-clinic personnel have found that some of their most valuable contributions to the handicapped child lie in simply giving the overwrought mother of such a child the wonderful luxury of an emotionally uninvolved listener.

Sometimes the help will take the form of equipment. A wheel chair, an over-bed table, exercise bars, or the tall, adjustable hospital bed, a commode to be kept downstairs to save steps—to have all this equipment available at the right time in the right sizes greatly eases a mother's load. If you live in or near a large city, you may wish to investigate the possibility of renting the more expensive items by the day, week, or month. If this valuable service is available in your vicinity, you will find it listed in the yellow pages of your phone directory under Hospital Equipment and Supplies. Although these rentals will vary widely in different areas, still, because a child outgrows such equipment so fast, renting is often more economical than investing.

There is much that a handy father can do in equipping a home for the easy care of an invalid or handicapped child. And just because it so often seems to these fathers that their only place in the scheme of things is to pay the ever-mounting bills, the chance to make a personal contribution in the form of a ramp or hand rails or a special tub seat may be a welcome one.

The mother of a different child may find her greatest help comes from equipment that has no connection with the child's handicap whatever, but rather in the labor-saving appliances that in other homes might be considered luxuries. A freezer, for instance, when trips to the store are major expeditions, is almost a necessity. And $400 invested in a washer-dryer may be worth more to the child and you and the rest of the family than thousands of dollars in psychiatric counseling and emotional rehabilitation.

The lowest prices will always be found at the supermarket, but for the home-bound mother the convenience of being able to phone her order into a nearby store for delivery at her door is well worth the higher prices she may meet. When it comes to shopping for other necessities, the "wish books" of generations of farm families—the mail-order catalogues—offer her armchair shopping that can make the difference between an ordered life and a frenzied one.

For the mother of the different child help is truly where she finds it, and no source should be overlooked. When a relative or neighbor murmurs, "Is there anything I can do?" the wise mother will seize upon the opportunity. Visiting a hospitalized child one afternoon a week, chauffeuring a child to the out-patient clinic, simply baby-sitting while you snatch a brief nap or treat yourself to an uninterrupted shampoo—all these are ways in which the thoughtful relative, friend, or neighbor can greatly ease the family faced with physical problems. Above all, family and friends can help by assuming that the mother's need for getting away from this child is as normal and natural and understandable as the need of the mother of any lively, happy youngster to get off by herself.

Great as is your need to be free of your child for a time, even greater is your child's need to be free from you. Not so much getting away from you as getting way from you *alone*. With different children we often operate on the premise that the fewer contacts they have with the rough world outside, the better.

We are not so apt to make this mistake with handicapped boys, for instinct tells us that to be too much with his mother is not the way for a boy to grow into a man. But daughters are different. If the physical effort involved in outings is very great, or if the few contacts she has had with the outside world have been painful ones, it seems only natural to take the line of least resistance and allow her to become a shadow of ourselves.

But no mother can be all things to a daughter. Children need contacts with adults of all types, and the more naturally and frequently they can meet with tradespeople, civil servants, and just plain strangers, the better rounded, the more nearly normal their lives will be.

In the case of the child enrolled in a clinic or receiving out-patient care in a hospital, her day may be so filled with contacts with other adults that any more social activity would be weary-ing. But with most handicapped children this is the most abnormal feature of their little world—the dearth of natural, easy, human contacts. The obvious answer, in a great many cases, is school. True, there are children whose handicaps preclude any normal school experience beyond that of a visiting teacher. But the number of these children is not nearly so large as is the number of children whose parents shy away from the idea of normal school experience.

"She's just not ready to be on her own yet," we hear a mother say when what she more frequently means is, "I am just not ready to let her go yet." Here, then, we come back to our basic premise: Do we really want a normal life for this little girl? If we do, then we must face the fact that what we call a normal life involves a constant weaning process from the day she is born. If we truly mean a normal life, then we must encourage her to take every step toward independence as she is ready for it, just as surely as the mother robin pushes the fledglings from the nest.

But if your doctor believes that your child is ready to start school, and if both you and she have made the necessary adjustments to the idea, one problem still remains: Shall she go to public school or a special school? In many cases no question will arise, for the physical condition or the mental ability of the child will preclude public school. But many a child with a very serious handicap has attended regular public-school classes, and has made a satisfactory adjustment. The parents who are in favor of public-school enrollments of the handicapped child will tell you that it is never too soon for the handicapped child to enter the "real world" where she is neither pampered nor cushioned. But it is a moot question where she will be most pampered. The one blind little girl enrolled in a nursery with thirty sighted children, or the little girl on crutches, who needs help with the more complex play equipment, often comes to be the center of loving attention and great maternal solicitude on the part of the children around them. Whoever originated the phrase, "the natural cruelty of little children," has never visited a school where one handicapped child was the problem and the concern and the delight of a classroom full of normal children.

On the other hand, if your daughter enters a class for other children who are handicapped in the same way and in the same degree that she is, she is accorded no special privileges, no special attention. For many a handicapped daughter, such a school offers her first experience in being just like anybody else. The experience is not always a pleasant one. It comes as a shock to a mother to find that her handicapped daughter frequently thinks of herself as someone very special. But it can hardly be surprising, when she has been surrounded by special attention and special care for as long as she can remember.

Any parent of any child needs always to be tempering extremes, bolstering the courage of her timid one while helping her young stoic to unbend, trying to relax her highly competitive daughter while she stiffens the spine of the one who is too easily led. But this particular phase of motherhood is more important in the life of a handicapped daughter for two reasons: first, the ordinary give and take of daily living in the world won't automatically smooth her to a happy medium, because her world is much more limited. Second, the world is less ruthless, more inclined to make allowances for the child it considers weaker than the average—a commendable attitude, but one which when carried to extremes can turn a handicapped child into a sissy, a Machiavellian schemer, or a tyrant.

When we were discussing minority groups, in the previous chapter, we mentioned the necessity for compensation. Here the same principle applies: to attain the same goals as a "normal" child the different daughter needs to be a little nicer, a little prettier, a little more talented; she needs to give more time and thought to her appearance, to attach more importance to the social graces, more emphasis on facility in sports, or in games popular with her crowd.

The little girl who was an Easter Seal poster child several years ago had a mother who understood the positive approach.

She bought a half-dozen of the cheapest crutches available, enameled them in luscious pastels, and trimmed them with glitter, sequins, and artificial flowers. What little girl wouldn't be proud?

Gay plaid and colored frames are available for glasses now, so inexpensive that a very small, very self-conscious girl can have a whole wardrobe of glasses. If Mother has a matching set, it's twice as exciting.

Hearing aids, so light that they are often prescribed for infants, are now nearly invisible.

Every year brings giant strides in the mechanical devices designed to help your daughter take her place beside her friends, yet anyone who designs or sells this equipment occasionally meets with indifference or downright hostility from those doctors whose thinking is geared to pure research.

"You can't mend broken bodies with gadgets," these medical men insist. True as that is, the fascinating new wealth of gadgets especially designed for specific requirements can minimize the differences between your daughter and the rest of the world.

Special clothing for the disabled, designed by Helen Cookman, under the sponsorship of the Institute of Physical Medicine and Rehabilitation of the New York University Medical Center, after three years of studying the needs of the handicapped, puts pretty clothes within the reach of even the child burdened by casts and braces.

But perhaps the most valuable gadgets of all are drive controls, the engineering miracles that put the family car at the disposal of the handicapped young person. For those of us who take walking for granted, it is hard to imagine the mobility, the sense of independence, the boost to ego and morale, represented by a driver's license.

"When I am behind the wheel of a car," a young arthritis victim told me exultantly, "nobody sees my legs. I'm a good driver and I know it, and when I'm driving I'm the equal of anybody else in the world!"

The equal of anybody else in the world. That is our goal, isn't it? If we can provide for our handicapped daughter enough of such moments, moments when she feels the equal of anyone else in the world, then we have fulfilled our place as mothers.

For a mother's role, complex though it is, is essentially this: to love our different daughter so wholesomely and without reservation that she grows up knowing that she will be a woman worthy of love.

If we can accept her just as she is, "differentness" and all, if she can accept herself as wholeheartedly, then the most tragic handicap can be reduced to a mere inconvenience in an otherwise triumphant and victorious life.

CHAPTER 12

Their Waking Hours

CALL it latent learning, or subliminal perception, or just call it living on a twenty-four-hour-a-day basis—call it what you will, I believe we have found a priceless cache of extra hours.

No, we haven't changed the calendar or the clock; we're still managing within the framework of the same old day, but we've discovered a secret about the minds of our girls. We've found that they are aware of their surroundings and of the atmosphere of their environment, not just during their waking hours, but twenty-four hours a day.

That's not, strictly speaking, a new concept. For years actors, students of foreign languages, and others whose success depends on their memories have known that the mind learns even when we seem to be asleep. Now, our girls may have no desire to commit to memory the third act of *Hamlet*, or to master the idioms of Swahili, but this same concept that is now helping to create for them a deeper and more meaningful family life can someday be a useful tool of their own motherhood. They will learn that they can solve a variety of parent-child conflicts, reach a troubled and frightened youngster, and give their children a greater sense of security than they would otherwise know. At least that's the way it seems to be working out at our house.

Latent learning the psychologists call this learning that takes place on the unconscious or subconscious level, but we've all had brushes with it in daily living, whether we called it by its impressive name or not.

You've noticed, for instance, that Susie sleeps fitfully, fretfully, when she's in an unfamiliar house, haven't you? Or that her sleep will be disturbed—though perhaps not quite broken —by a fire siren, or the roar of a train, or a family "discussion" that got out of bounds.

We learned that in our first year of our first baby, and we learned it—as we have had to learn so many things about the first child—the hard way.

We were living in Washington, and it was spring. Spring along the Potomac is a special spring, different from any other anywhere, and it seemed strange that Lindy didn't respond to the sunlight and the greenness and the softness in the air. Instead, she was pale and jumpy. And while she wasn't losing weight, she wasn't gaining any, either.

Our apartment was in one of those old row houses so typical of the older sections of the capital, with our kitchen window and the kitchen window of the house next door nearly touching. During the day we didn't mind, but every night, as regularly as a scheduled boxing match, the couple next door began their evening bout. It was strictly main-event caliber, too, with nothing barred, including outcries and crockery.

My husband and I tried to mind it less by treating the whole thing as a joke; with housing so hard to find, there was little else we could do. And at least, we often reassured each other, they waited until the baby was asleep.

And yet that's all that was wrong with Lindy. We didn't find it out until the hot weather set in, and Lindy, paradoxically, began to gain weight. In the worst of the heat we had slipped into the habit of putting her to bed in her carriage and walking with her through the city. Even the oven-hot streets were less oppressive than our little apartment, and as we pushed the carriage through the dusk, past Union Station, past the fountains painted with colored lights, into the green lawn around the Capitol building, small fresh wisps of wind would sometimes stir.

If it was the night for a band concert from the broad white steps, we would spread a sheet on the grass, settle Lindy on it, and lie beside her, listening to the music, watching the stars and the softly glowing dome. Lindy never woke, even when we laid her back in the carriage and made our way home through the dark, silent streets. She seldom woke, even when we lifted her into her own crib in her own quiet room—quiet, because by then the fracas next door was over! Of course—it was as simple as that!

Well, we found another apartment, and fast, once we realized how deeply, though unconsciously, Lindy was being affected by the unpleasantness.

Not only was our new neighborhood free of neighbors who threw crockery at their spouses, it yielded new friends who taught us still more about the strange ways of the mind asleep. Rosemary and Don were amused to think that we considered our theory original. Months before, when their daughter went back to bedwetting again after she started kindergarten, Rosemary tried going into her girl's room just before the parents went to bed each night, sitting on the side of her child's bed and talking quietly to her.

"You're going to stay dry tonight," she would say softly.

"Won't that be comfortable? You're going to stay dry and warm and comfortable all night long."

Rosemary kept a chart of the nights she did this and of the nights she forgot, or was too late, and sure enough—the chart showed it worked as simply as a charm. Too simply, it seemed to her. She had a theory that it wasn't the words but just her presence, the soothing sound of her voice, that was getting through to her daughter and helping to assuage whatever inner turmoil had brought on this return to wet sheets. And she proved her point—when Rosemary just talked, stroked her child's head, told her what a good girl she was, and how much they both loved her, she stayed dry, though not a word was spoken about wetting. What's more, although it had never been mentioned in these nocturnal monologues, their daughter stopped biting her nails, too.

Another friend, who found that her little girl was reacting unhappily to a new brother despite every possible effort by her parents, tried this nighttime approach with heartwarming results. Each evening, when the demanding new infant was temporarily bedded down and the housework was finished (or as nearly finished as it ever can be where there's a new baby), she sat by her sleeping toddler's bed and talked. Nothing witty or erudite, just everyday talk about the fun they had enjoyed that day, or the things they would do together tomorrow. It's not *what* you say, apparently, it's the sound of your voice, and your nearness.

Just two years ago a far more serious problem reared its head in our own home. No, latent learning didn't exactly solve it—at least not directly—but it helped.

We had suddenly come to see that through a whole series of circumstances and of those mistakes which even the most well-meaning parents make we had been giving Lindy, our eldest child, more time and attention than Laurie received. Once we realized what we were doing, we did an abrupt about-face, making sure that Laurie got more cuddling, more talk, and more time. We also cut down sharply on several special privileges that Lindy had gradually come to feel were her due. I remember how noble we felt, how sure we were that we were doing the right thing.

Lindy reacted to the new order of things with surprisingly mature acceptance, but the behavior of Laurie, who should have felt happier than she had for months, bewildered us. It began with sly pinches and pokes at Lindy when they were alone. Lindy, outraged, would hit her back, and the battle was on. But they have always done their full share of sisterly quarreling; what disturbed us was that Laurie consistently denied these misdeeds. Lying was something new for Laurie, usually so open, so loving, so trustingly truthful. We knew that most children have their lapses from truthfulness—Lindy and our toddler, Joyce, had had some—but Laurie! It all seemed so out of character. And it got worse; soon Lindy missed money, and we found it in Laurie's drawer. Through it all Laurie would first insist, even when faced with the proof, that she hadn't been the culprit. When that happened, we always sent both of them to their rooms—again we were so sure we were being fair and wise—until the guilty party was willing to tell the truth. Finally, after storming and weeping, Laurie would eventually come out and sullenly admit that her big sister had told the truth. And Lindy, with the charity only the wronged can afford, would always forgive her.

All this time we hadn't the heart to punish Laurie too severely because she was so obviously tormented and miserable. Our sunny Laurie had become so morose that she hardly spoke to us, and drew away sharply when we put our arms around her or kissed her good night. Heart-to-heart talks didn't help; Laurie's only explanation was a sullen, "I don't know why I did it."

My husband and I were frantic, naturally, for we knew that somehow we were failing her. Writing of it now, it all looks so obvious, but at the time it was frightening and bewildering and it was poisoning our once-happy family life.

The climax came one evening when our eldest girl found her room a shambles—books crayoned, toys broken, pictures torn. After the recriminations and the crying died down, after Laurie had been soundly spanked and sent off to bed, after the whole house had settled down to an uneasy nighttime quiet, I tiptoed into Lindy's room. She had been very understanding, and I was proud of her. I sat down on the side of the bed and reached out my hand to stroke her forehead, but she jumped when I touched her and, still asleep, retreated to the far side of the bed. I tried again; again she jerked away.

I crossed the hall to Laurie's room. Asleep, she looked so different from her daytime self. With her eyes still puffed and red from crying and streaks of tears drying on her cheeks, still hiccuping little sobs, she looked like the dear child she had always been in the past—she looked so very open and guileless and, well, she looked angelic.

There in the darkness and quiet, alone with my sleeping daughters, I experienced a sudden flash of insight. I could only stand there, looking down at Laurie, trying to face the enormity of the injustice her father and I had done her. For I knew then, somehow I just *knew*, that her big sister, caught up in rebellion and resentment too big to handle, had been spinning a web of lies around Laurie. Looking back I saw that the evidence had always been too pat, too readily supplied by Lindy.

We knew we were in above our depth, so we turned to the Child Guidance Clinic in our city. The psychologist there helped us all to understand where we had gotten off the track. And he helped us see that even an hour of being shut in her room alone was to exuberant, active Laurie a form of torture that could force her to admit to anything just to get out. He helped us a great deal, but it was those quiet moments in the night, just sitting there feeling close to them both, that first opened my eyes. Is it any wonder that I declare to anyone who will listen that this principle of latent learning is a two-way exchange in which the child is not always the student? Sometimes you can see more clearly in the dark.

But latent learning can be our foe as well as our ally. The way we react to any sudden nighttime crisis will leave a deep impression and that impression may not always be a pleasant one.

Nightmares, for instance. None of us enjoys being roused from a warm bed, but the way we respond when our child wakes shaken and sobbing from the dark shadow of a dream is so important. No weariness, no impatience should be great enough to overbalance the terrible need a child has for us then. Need for comfort, need to tell us all about it, perhaps, but above all the overwhelming need for our simply being awake and *there*.

Nights of illness, too, are a challenge to our patience and wisdom. But if we meet the challenge, our vigil at the bedside of a sick child can create memories more lasting and cherished than any rapport we can build by day. Medical corpsmen on any battlefield know how many desperately wounded men have called up a picture of their mothers tending them when they were sick children, to bridge a space of time too terrible to face alone.

We are women now, and we are expected to be strong and stoic however bad we feel. It's too late for us to return to the lamplight and the gentle hands of our own mother's nursing, but we can become part of the ancient ritual with our own daughters. And in time they will take up the lamp, part of the endless procession. Sometimes in the press of daily living we almost lose touch with our children; all of us sometimes feel that we can scarcely remember how it feels to be a child. But in sickness we remember. A feverish child holds tight to our hand and we know exactly what she feels, what she needs. Our backs may ache and our eyes grate with weariness, but we remember what it means to a sick child to know that we are watching over her or at least will come at her first faint call—remember that she needs that sure knowledge as much as she needs any medication.

The same thing is true of the child plagued by fears, and here's an area where latent learning can work miracles. If your daughter is afraid of storms, or sirens, or high winds, try this—go to her *before* she wakes, the instant you hear the sound she dreads. She hears it, too, but she hears your voice and feels your hand, and nine out of ten times she won't wake at all. (Of course you will be working to still her dread during the daytime, too—taking her to visit your firehouse, perhaps with Daddy, climbing on the great shiny engines, meeting the firemen as people, even being allowed to sound the siren just for a moment, or sitting by the window, the fearful one cuddled safe in your lap, laughing together at the noisy, rollicking storm, trying to guess just how long after the lightning the thunder will crash, or seeing if she can drown out the boom with her drum or by banging on the dishpan with the big basting spoon.) But we are speaking here of nighttime, and our experience—and our friends have had the same results—shows that she will lose the fear itself surprisingly quickly, for now that sound is associated with a pleasant sensation.

But the half-awake, half-asleep experiences of our children's lives aren't like spinach, to be administered for the "good" they can do. These hours are for fun, too. Of course children belong in their own comfortable beds, in their own quiet rooms. Most of the time. But a child who never has any nighttime adventures misses a lot of memories. For it's that half-asleep state that makes her memories magic.

Our eight-year-old has had eight Christmas trees and seen hundreds of others, yet there never comes a Christmas that she doesn't say, "Remember the tree I saw that night?"

We were living in a furnished room, in a shabby, rundown neighborhood that leaned heavily to other furnished rooms.

One night just before Christmas the elderly woman across the hall knocked at our door and asked shyly whether the little girls would like to see her tree. She hadn't put one up for years, now that she was all alone, she explained, but this year, what with children in the house and all . . .

Well, both the girls had just dropped off to sleep, but neither their father nor I could have told that dear old person that they couldn't be disturbed. My husband took one child and I took the other and we carried them, wrapped in blankets, across the hall.

It was a small tree, sparse of branch, but it was hung with delicate fairytale ornaments that must have been cherished through a whole lifetime of Christmases. There were tiny spun-glass birds, little golden trumpets, great glass bubbles with snow scenes imprisoned inside. And real lighted wax candles!

Laurie, then still a baby, refused to wake, but when Lindy, just about four, opened her eyes and saw that tree, she was simply enchanted. Such an expression of awe and joy and wonder crossed her face that all three grownups were a little misty-eyed. Other trees have come along, larger, more beautiful perhaps, but she still remembers the one she found in that magic waking moment.

Laurie's favorite nighttime memory is of the night we dragged the rocker out onto the front lawn and watched a shower of shooting stars. Neither of us remembers how it happened—whether she just wandered downstairs, or whether I woke her to see the exciting sky—but oh! how she remembers that night.

Every fifth of July our girls are cranky, quarrelsome, impossible to live with. That's because on the night of the Fourth of July they never get enough sleep.

You see, every Fourth of July we drive out to the Sauerweins' for a gathering of the clan and an all-day picnic. Their back field slopes down to the edge of the park, giving us a grandstand seat for the municipal fireworks—the climax of the day.

When all the hide-and-seek and tag and horseshoes are over; when every corner of the barn has been explored; when everyone has eaten too many hot dogs and too many charred marshmallows; when all the sparklers have glittered and then spluttered out in the dusk—then the children fall asleep. They go by ages, dropping off wherever they make the mistake of slowing down for a moment. The very littlest end up on the lap of one grandmother or another, while the middle-sized children curl up on the swing or the glider or under a picnic table. By the time the music from the distant bandstand blows away and the fireworks begin, all but the oldest must be shaken back to consciousness or they would miss the whole gorgeous spectacle.

Last year it was so hard for Laurie to wake up, and she just couldn't stay awake, but kept dozing off, until I felt guilty. "Perhaps," I said on the way home, "perhaps we shouldn't go again until the girls are older. It just upsets their bedtime schedule, and what do the little ones get out of it, after all?"

Well, we found out. This winter, when the art teacher asked Laurie and her classmates to paint the most beautiful thing each of them could think of, Laurie brought home a vivid splash of riotous blues and yellows and oranges and reds against a solid black background. No hypocrite, I—I asked her point-blank to tell me what the picture meant.

This orange circle was the campfire, I was told, with the fire burned down to embers. That was the big gray farmhouse sleeping in the background. The barn didn't show, she explained solemnly, because it was black and the sky was black, too, but it was there all right, and there was an owl sitting on the ridgepole. (I would have sworn she was sound asleep when Bob called to us to look at that old owl.)

These were the children, those were the grownups sitting around the fire, and that was the Sauerweins' big pit bull, Major, asleep on the steps. The really vivid colors were the fireworks, *of course* (mothers can be so dense!). Those wavy lines? Why, that's the way the voices sound when you're very, very sleepy.

So I guess we'll go back next year. There are some things more important than a good night's sleep. The experiences a child meets on the edge of sleep stay with them long after daytime adventures fade.

These experiences will stay with them long after childhood is past, and, because they remember, they will provide the bounty of this twenty-four-hour living for their children, too.

They will grow into motherhood knowing that there are no sleeping hours, really, but only waking hours, in greater or less degrees, that every youngster is the product of many experiences she may not consciously remember, because each of us lives and grows and learns and changes twenty-four hours a day.

If our pace is hectic, surely by the time our daughters are mothers theirs will be more so. If present trends continue, with more widespread employment of women, with a greater exodus to the suburbs resulting in more and yet more commuting fathers, even less time may be available for families to be together. In that case, one of the most useful tools we can give our daughters will be the concept of round-the-clock family life.

Because for busy, harried parents, who sometimes find the days too short for all the affection and "togetherness" they would like to achieve, all twenty-four hours offer a priceless opportunity.

CHAPTER **13**

What Are We Going to Do About Grandmother?

WHEN a rabble-rouser or a demagogue lashes a mob to frenzy with loaded, emotion-charged words, intelligent women refuse to be taken in. But when we trick ourselves with loaded words, we're not so quick to sense the trap.

Take "grandmother." Now there's a silver-haired word, all pink cheeks, ample lap, sunny, fragrant kitchen, gingerbread, and milk. Just let the grandmothers in our families fail to measure up to this picture of placid conformity and we feel somehow betrayed.

But even a hundred years ago, when the avenues of expression open to grandmothers were limited, there were enough wiry, peppery old ladies, and stately, formal dowagers to dis-

courage generalization. Today, when Grandmother's hair
shade may be mad mauve and her profession range from
housewife through school-bus driver to city councilman, there
are as many types of grandmothers as there are grandmothers.
And each of them can be the best thing that ever happened to
a little girl.

There's not a grandmother anywhere, however old-
fashioned, or uneducated, or eccentric she may be, who does
not have great gifts to give a grandaughter. On the other hand,
there is no grandmother, however successful and busy and
celebrated she may be, who will not be the richer for the gifts
her granddaughter can bring to her. It is the very reciprocity
of their need that makes the relationship so meaningful.

The gift of roots. Well over thirty-one million Americans
each year pack up their worldly goods and move; more than
ten and a half million of these moves are long-distance ones—
to another county or state. And each year the nomad trend
increases. In such a time of wandering, our children need roots.

Particularly our daughters need roots, for they will be the
mothers in the equally rootless future, and the solidity and
permanence of the family have been a mother's assignment
since families began.

Our daughters are surrounded by frenetic change. Yesterday's open field is today's shopping plaza; today's shopping
plaza is tomorrow's garden-apartment development. More
than any past generations, our young people today need their
grandparents' houses which in so many cases remain always on
the same streets, in the same towns, no matter how often the
child's own home changes.

But the most nourishing roots go deeper than one generation. Stories of Grandpa's early days, stories of, "Why, I mind
when that whole section was a pasture, with a peach orchard
up there on the hill; Elbertas, they were," bring home to even
a little girl a reminder of the continuity of family life and the
endless flow of time.

We Americans, so quick to condemn snobbery and special privilege, are apt to ridicule the many organizations based on genealogies and the war records of generations past. Yet to a child all this is immeasurably consoling. It is convincing evidence of the comforting continuity of the family and of her own place in the world.

If the memories cross an ocean or two, so much the better. It is a sad fact that the first generation of children born of immigrant parents nearly always reject the old ways. Like angry adolescents they throw off all remnants of the despised and "inferior" customs of their parents. But the second generation, unhampered by emotion, soaks up the old-world atmosphere eagerly. What child, raised on *Muckey, Muchke, Melele* or *O! Tannenbaum* ever forgets them? Grandparents from another country can, if we let them, give from their hearts to make their granddaughters richer by far than children with only a single cultural heritage.

The gift of wings. For daughters as for flowers, roots are only a means to higher ends. And when it comes to reaching toward the sun, the older generation can give our girls wings. To a proud grandmother nothing is impossible for her granddaughter. Did the child do well at the dance-school rehearsal? She will surely be a prima ballerina. Is she beginning to show promise of better-than-average features? She will be a great beauty, a breaker of hearts. It can be irritating to us, these flights of wishful thinking, so much so that we sometimes take joy in pricking the balloon with barbed realities. But really, now, doesn't every little girl need someone to dream with? In a world where her parents are constantly remodeling her every trait, where school becomes more demanding at each grade level, how safe and warm to have one person to whom she is a princess without flaw!

In a material sense, too, grandmothers can help our daughters grow wings. Even if a grandparent is living on a pension, older people often have remarkable habits of thrift, and get extraordinary joy from the pleasure of giving gifts whether or not they can easily afford them. And even if they can, their gestures are not always properly welcomed. It can become a very complex problem, this question of how much we can allow our parents to buy for our children without harm to the delicate balance of family relationships. It's a problem which may profitably be talked over with an objective outsider, such as a family service agency or a marriage counselor. Because important though it is for each family unit to stand on its own feet, it is cruel waste to deprive our children of advantages and deprive their grandparents of the joys of giving, if it is only our own emotion that is creating the conflict.

But children are not always on the receiving end of all this giving. Life takes on a new meaning for a grandmother who is taken into a grandchild's life.

Many an older woman is understandably reluctant to adopt styles or colors or hair-dos or make-up that might be considered overly youthful or extreme. But the canny fashion advice of an interested, understanding adolescent may give her just the incentive she needs to update her appearance and thereby boost her self-confidence.

Even a toddler—or an infant—can widen the older woman's world. Especially if a grandmother is a shy, retiring person, or if she has been transplanted into a new neighborhood, she will discover that pushing a baby carriage again is an automatic conversation starter among her new neighbors. And there is nothing quite so certain to transform two strangers into acquaintances as sharing a bench in the playground while they oversee their toddler-age grandchildren.

It's an obvious fact that there is often more room for the older generation in your daughter's life than there is in yours. That's the third contribution these two generations offer each other.

The gift of time. Grandparents have so much time. It lies like a yoke across their shoulders, bending them under its weight. It's ironic, but it's tragic, too. On the one hand we have millions of harassed young mothers, trying to do fifty hours' work in twenty-four, with never quite enough time, and on the other hand we have multitudes of grandmothers figuratively rocking on a shelf, longing for a taste of that sweet confusion again.

Last fall Chatham, New Jersey, inaugurated an educational innovation that may start a whole new era of exploiting all available grandmother power. There, grandparents are pressed into service as volunteer part-time school helpers or teacher associates. Although still an experiment, the results have been gratifying, not only in developing more relaxed teachers and enthusiastic children, but in improving the morale of the oldsters.

This is the unexpected dividend when we impose a bit on the older generation and borrow from their greater store of time—the grandparents benefit, too. No less an authority than Dr. Robert T. Monroe, director of the Boston Age Center's Health Division, looking at it from a physician's standpoint, has this to say:

"It is becoming increasingly clear that it is a good health rule to live within the upper limits of physical and mental capabilities."

So lean a little! To attend to all the many facets of a daughter's life as thoroughly as we would wish is more than a full-time job. Especially if we handle it all ourselves. But if only one or two of these functions can be delegated to a grandmother, how much easier our day becomes. Grandmothers are wonderful teachers of sewing or cooking or gardening or German or square dancing. They can be so much more patient because they have so much more time. Grandparents make wonderful dance chaperones and sorority sponsors, and are often grateful to have been asked, not accepting reluctantly as a busy mother may.

Grandmothers have more time for excursions than mothers

have and often they have more inclination, too. Especially for the retired grandparent who finds the hours long, a trip to the zoo or the farmer's market or downtown with a wide-eyed child gives meaning to the day.

Shut-in grandmothers can be delightful tea-party partners, or storytellers. And I wonder what percentage of children of every generation learned their first card games playing with Grandmother? There is a book by Edith Young and Phyllis Cerf, *Complete Family Fun Book*, that you might unobtrusively contribute to your daughters' grandmothers to help them in developing a rewarding relationship with their granddaughters.

Even if the grandparents in your family live miles away, their time can bring joy to your daughter. What little girl doesn't love to have the mailman bring her a real letter? And almost as much fun is writing a letter. A bulletin board such as the one we described in the chapter about fathers might become a very comforting substitute for near-at-hand grandparents. Then, too, faraway grandmothers are such fun to visit. A little girl will usually stay overnight or for a vacation at Grandmother's house long before she is grown up enough to visit anywhere else alone.

Some young parents who have no parents living—not even faraway ones—feel so strongly about the advantages of grandparents that they are "adopting" them. Many homes for the aged are organizing adoption services whereby a young family adopts—with no legal connotations, of course—one of the lonely, family-less old people on their rolls. The "grandmother" basks in the simple joy of letters, family snapshots, small gifts, Sunday-afternoon drives, and holiday dinners; the "grandchild" gains all the many benefits contact with all ages will impart.

All recent research seems to indicate that the most complex and demanding role our daughters will face is that of becoming, someday, elder citizens themselves. Nothing will do so much to prepare them for that future as time spent in a complete, three-generation-family situation.

Not that all grandparents are an unadulterated joy.

There is, for one thing, that widespread complaint that grandparents, if entrusted with their children's children, will stuff them with sweets and satiate them with an excess of worthless little toys. Now I have no intention of defending the practice, for there is no surer, quicker way to undermine the disciplined and orderly existence we strive to give our daughters, but I do maintain that such excesses are not so much malicious as they are pathetic. The grandmother who gives so intemperately of candy and gimcracks does so because she believes she has nothing of real value to give. When she is given a role of importance in her granddaughter's life, when she comes to know intimately all the child's interests and unique capabilities, when she is allowed to play a vital part in purchasing plans and training decisions and long-range family projects, she often becomes as practical and sensible as we could wish. Girls who are to be the emotional trustees of their husbands' and children's lives can't know this deep human need too early.

This is only one of the problems a grandmother may pose. There are some who find fault endlessly, some who play favorites, some who fasten upon an impressionable young granddaughter and feed on her sympathy or on her strength and vigor. But love works miracles at any age, and the number of cantankerous, contentious old women who have been transformed into lovable human beings by the fondness of an affectionate granddaughter is beyond calculation.

In those rare cases where a problem grandmother appears to be beyond reformation, I submit that she is better than no grandmother at all. It might even be argued that one of the five benefits of grandparents is:

The gift of differences. In their very early years little girls inhabit a black-and-white world. Parents are perfect. On television, the good men ride white horses and are clean-shaven, the bad men wear mustaches or a three-day stubble of beard and ride black horses.

Unfortunately, the world outside is not so neatly arranged. A little girl soon discovers that the playmate who is so much fun to be with sometimes tells lies to get her into trouble. The teacher who is so stern and forbidding makes new words come alive and dance across the primer page. Suddenly the black and white are all mixed up together and the child is mixed up, too.

But a girl who has been close to two other generations all her life, and has listened to the give and take, the discussions, the criticisms that are bound to arise from time to time, can absorb this inconsistency with aplomb. She grows up knowing that none of us is perfect, a highly useful piece of information if she is to be the mentor for her family someday. More important, she learns that there can be differences without division, hostility without hate.

Most small children believe that their parents are just about perfect. That may come as a shock, but all the experts say it's true. No wonder the young child who quarrels with her parents is sick with guilt inside, certain that she must be in the wrong. But when she finds that each question has *three* sides, she's no longer the villain.

Above all, the discovery that the most important adults in her life can disagree violently on a dozen issues, yet remain a fond and solid family group, is blessed reassurance. *You* argue with *your* parents, yet you all love each other—suddenly those hostile thoughts she has sometimes harbored seem harmless and natural enough.

In a slightly different way differences between you and her grandparents can teach a child tolerance. If superstitions, lower standards of grammar, different food habits, or frequently (in this age of transition) differences in religious emphasis, are encountered for the first time in her own family circle, among people she loves and admires, she will be prepared, in future encounters with strangers, to realize that *dif-ference* doesn't automatically imply *inferiority*.

Where the standards of grandparents differ drastically from our own there's bound to be worry about bad influences. But let's be painfully honest: are our differences really so impor-tant? It has always seemed to me that most such complaints arise, not against grandmothers, but against mothers-in-law. Perhaps if we could change our mental terminology, we might be able to see the differences between the generations with less emotion. To call our mother-in-law "mother-in-love," as Mary Martin does, would be a bit too saccharine for most of us. But some change might be an improvement, for it is vital that we think of her first and foremost as our daughter's grandmother.

Whether or not we get on with a mother-in-law or mother is our problem. But it becomes very much our daughter's prob-lem when we can't get along with her grandmother. She needs a grandmother and a grandfather just as much as she needs a mother and a father, although in different degree and for different reasons. We toss the word "sacrifices" around very lightly, often speaking of "a mother's sacrifice." Well, here's a sacrifice really worth making. Are we big enough women, are we clever enough women, to give our daughters the advan-tages of grandparents?

And what advantages there are, even when major differences in background or way of living seem to present obstacles.

If our parents live on a drastically simpler scale than ours, our daughter can learn from them the virtues of simplicity and thrift. She can learn to appreciate plain foods, inexpensive pleasures. She will learn a whole different way of housekeeping, because different tools are at her disposal—an opportunity we've already lauded in an earlier chapter.

If our parents live on a considerably more elaborate scale than ours, then our daughters are offered a chance to explore a world of luxury, beauty, and opportunities that they might not otherwise discover for several years. Perhaps life at Grandmother's house is lived on a more formal plane, but who will say that exposure to fine manners is a handicap?

Parents who still cling to an old-world background can provide our children with more than the gift of roots we mentioned earlier—they provide adventure. What is more exciting than holiday festivals in the old neighborhood, visits to exotic foreign food stalls at the city markets, or church services in a foreign tongue?

A grandparent who now faces fewer family demands upon her time has often turned to volunteer community services, to politics, or to worth-while clubs. Sharing these interests, her granddaughter glimpses a vital world that her mother, busy with myriad home duties, may not be able to show her.

Another problem mothers face is that it is not easy to share, or even to understand, the enthusiasm of a daughter who is outstandingly talented, unless her talents lie in the same field as our own. But she may have a grandparent who speaks the same language—be it art, music, or whatever—to the great enrichment of them both. Quite often what we decry as favoritism on a grandmother's part is no more than this, simply a reaching out to touch a talent or an interest or a trait which she recognizes and understands. If we have one daughter who is not getting what we believe is her fair share of attention from her grandmother, the remedy often lies in developing or creating such common ground.

A moment's thought will usually prove that the favored child is the one who most resembles—in appearance and tastes—the older woman's own children. This may be reprehensible but it certainly is understandable. By favorably comparing the youngest generation and our own, and by pointing out small characteristic family resemblances and tendencies wherever we can discover them, the neglected grandchild can often be shown to her grandmother in a new light.

Certainly so rewarding a relationship is well worth an effort on our part; no adult and no child ever has too much love.

The more people a daughter has to love her, the happier she'll be. I'm sure it's more than coincidence that the most outgoing, loving child in our own family is the one who, from her first weeks, was cared for regularly by three adoring older women and two doting teenagers.

No, it's not always easy to get along with grandparents, but I'm convinced that it is we mothers who have the power to mold the three generations into a big, cheerful, easy-going, happy family. Even in the difficult case of grandparents living with their children, it is the young women who set the tone.

It's never the best solution—three generations living together—but sometimes it's the *only* solution. There have been so many authoritative treatises on living happily with an older generation in the home that I'm certainly not going to try to cover it here. (An excellent pamphlet is listed at the end of this book.) This isn't a book about grandparents, anyway, it's a book about daughters. And although there are many disadvantages a girl must face when a grandparent moves in, there are so many advantages she gains. If we accentuate the positive, stress the advantages, our children will follow our lead.

But it may be the disadvantages that prove to be the greatest advantage of all. For if there is one way we are failing our children today, it is in training for responsibility, for duty. "Choose the path of duty and habit will make it pleasant," is another of those proverbs whose comfort I swear by in times of crisis. And it is true of us and of our children.

If we accept the extra member of our family grudgingly, she will be a burden; if we welcome her, she may prove to be a blessing. At first you may all have to pretend (your new guest may be pretending, too, remember), but in time your cheerful acceptance will be real. Given time, the mask will come to be the face itself.

Recently I read a sermon by the Rev. Harry W. Eberts, minister of the First Presbyterian Church of Marietta, Ohio, which flooded an ancient precept with new light.

"If a man compels you to go with him one mile, go with him two." How often I've heard and even quoted that difficult advice of Jesus. But I never really understood it until the Rev. Mr. Eberts filled in the political climate of those times for me. The Jews were in much the same relation to the Romans then as the Hungarians and East Germans are to the Russians today. One hated symbol of their humiliation was the law whereby any Roman courier bearing official dispatches could draft any Jew he saw to carry his heavy dispatch case for one mile. It was a hated task, a mark of slavery, and a man naturally counted out every step of the mile and at the end of it resentfully set down his burden to hurry home. But then Jesus proposed this simple but startling possibility: convert duty to free will, slavery to triumph. A courier can force you to go with him one mile, but if at the end of that mile you choose to carry your burden another mile, you are no longer a slave! It's a thrilling concept, isn't it? One that we can apply to any situation.

Forced to take an older relative into a home, we can shoulder the burden bitterly, or we can welcome it wholeheartedly, giving love where only acceptance is required. Suddenly it's not a burden, but a challenge. We can find sensible, cheerful ways to make everyone happier. Perhaps a nursery school for that noisy preschooler during Grandmother's nap time. Or the "day care" plan that many homes for the elderly provide, enabling the aged to spend their days at the home, their evenings with their families, may offer a solution. We may have to make changes in our sleeping arrangements, our menus, and our thinking, but we will rediscover the triumphant joy that comes of not just doing, but embracing our duties.

Our girls, having discovered that joy, will never be quite so selfish or ingrown again and they will come face to face with the fifth great gift grandparents can give:

The gift of need. It is not often that young girls are truly needed. We give them so much, and there's so little they can give. But grandmothers get lonely, they misplace their glasses, their balls of yarn roll under sofas, they can't read the fine print in the phone book any longer, so a girl can contribute.

Because mothers are needed so much that it swamps us, it's hard to imagine what it would be like not to be needed enough.

But daughters know.

So do grandparents.

They need each other.

CHAPTER 14

Love and Little Girls

SUGAR and spice ... and puppy dogs' tails, *that* is what little girls are *really* made of. If this book gives the impression that ours are any different, it's not because I have any illusions about them or because I'm trying to deceive you; it's only that I have a wholesome fear of the power of words to influence a child's behavior.

A very wise teacher once confided that each year she sought out the most unattractive little girl in her class and whispered in her ear, "I declare, child, you get prettier every day." The results—and they were dramatic—are exactly the same in the area of behavior.

I admit that this idea of proclaiming right out loud that I have three good little girls is disgracefully old-fashioned. There's a whole new cult arising among the mothers of the nation, a cult with Dennis the Menace their patron saint and caustic wit their creed. Twenty years ago it was considered quite respectable to love your children openly; twenty years from now, if fads come a full circle, it may even be fashionable. But this is now, and it certainly puts the sentimental mother on the spot.

Admittedly, I'm the type who saves first baby shoes, whose closets are crammed with blobs of kindergarten color, valentines that shower down dried paste, and the plaster-of-Paris handprints each child in turn bore proudly home from second grade. Sentimental. Hopelessly, unfashionably sentimental. But I honestly believe I'm right.

Now you take this morning.

"How I envy you those sweet little girls," my neighbor sighed. Now I know just as well as you do that the code called for me to roll my eyes, strike my brow, and groan, "Sweet! You should see them when they're inside!"

But I just couldn't do it. "Thanks," I murmured lamely. "How's Sandy?"

"You mean the monster? Let me tell you what that little demon did this morning!"

Call it loyalty, if you like, or preservation of dignity, but I feel there's an element of betrayal in such a flippant dismissal of a child's pride.

I've come to dread the bright red banner across a new magazine that promises "Complete in this issue—another hilarious article by Shirley Jackson," or Jean Kerr, or Eleanor Goulding Smith—the talented oracles of this new religion. It's not that I don't enjoy them—I laugh and laugh until the tears come. But I can always count on my husband, eying the rip in the living-room rug or the threadbare seat of his old winter overcoat, to stare thoughtfully at the magazine and then at me.

"You know," he'll finally venture, "I'll bet you could write something like this."

And it's impossible to explain why my sentimental nature foils me every time.

That week we spent at the farm was a classic example. From New Year's on I kept dropping little seeds. "Every child should have the memory of summer on the farm," I pointed out. "And you could drive up for the weekend.

"Best of all, it wouldn't have to cost us a cent," was the clincher! I had it all worked out: two city children and one city baby turned loose for a whole week on an unsuspecting rural countryside were bound to furnish enough hilarious material to beguile an editor. "Why, one article could pay for the whole project," I insisted.

Only it didn't work out that way.

Oh, they had their offbeat adventures, and I made copious notes about Lindy and the dead frog, and Laurie trying to bait her fishhook with an extremely live worm, and brave tomboy Lindy face to face at last with a real horse. But I delayed too long.

By the time we got back home to the typewriter, the funny things, the brittle, ridiculous things, had faded. All that remained sharp and clear were the pleasant times. The peaceful golden evenings when we sat on the rough plank steps and watched the milking, smelling the strong, clean, cow smell, listening to the deep cow voices and the rattling and clanking of their stanchions. Or the rainy afternoon when we let the baby nap right where she fell asleep in the hayloft. Or seeing a county fair again, really seeing it, through the children's eyes. Or the night we sat on the front porch, rocking, waiting for the storm to cross the ring of hills, listening to the thunder and the silence—the good things.

It seems to be a family failing—this emphasis on the best about each other, rather than the worst. Our girls have the same unpredictable, selective memory.

"What is the nicest hour of Sunday?" Laurie's Sunday-school teacher asked her—a leading question if ever I heard one! But Laurie blithely missed her cue and answered, "When we first wake up, when it's real early and we bring in the paper and the bag from the baker's and all jump into Mummy and Daddy's bed to eat pecan buns and read the funnies." She's right—it's sticky, but it's nice. And I'm grateful that she remembers Sundays by that hour, rather than by the later hectic one, when it's already past time to leave for Sunday school, and Lindy discovers the hole in the thumb of her white glove and I can't find the lesson plan for my class, and we can't find Joyce's left shoe.

You see, it's all a matter of emphasis.

Instead of remembering all the times they bicker and fight and squabble among themselves, I'd rather remember the times I've watched from the window as they started down the snowy street, little red mitten tucked trustingly in blue wool glove and wool glove resting in white bunny-fur mitten.

Only the warm memories are worthy of heart room. If I have any philosophy of child raising, that just about sums it up.

The warm memories are there, in nearly every experience; some just take a little more digging than others. Writers write about, cartoonists quip about, and for years I have moaned about the ordeal of taking the children downtown. And make no mistake, it *is* an ordeal. And the absolute, tragic, rock-bottom nadir of that ordeal is taking the children on a visit to Santa Claus.

"Tomorrow I'm taking Laurie downtown to see Santa Claus," I announced this December, at one memorable breakfast.

"How about me?" wailed Lindy.

"You're too big," I answered.

"How about me?" wailed Joyce.

"You're too little."

Their father looked up from his eggs. "Now that doesn't seem very fair," he protested.

"Well," I countered sweetly, "perhaps you could get an afternoon off and we could all . . ."

"Your mother is quite right, girls," he stated firmly, turning his attention hurriedly back to his eggs.

It turned out to be a day of freezing rain and sleet, of course, but I had Laurie wear her lined blue jeans instead of snow pants, so we could eliminate one step in the dress-undress-dress-undress process. Thanks to that foresighted wisdom, all I had to hold while we stood in line were my coat and purse and scarf and gloves, and Laurie's coat and hat and sweater and mittens and scarf, and a comic book, and the present for Grandmother, and the balloon with a snowman inside that Santa's elf had provided. In spite of the desultory stirrings of a little electric fan on the wall, the store was hot and my feet hurt and I tried to lean wearily, but there's just so much support in a loop of velvet rope.

We progressed to the throne, finally, and of course it wasn't really worth all the trouble. It never is, is it? Laurie forgot what she was going to ask for. Dressed in her old blue jeans, there was no point in having her picture taken, so Santa didn't seem to care very much what she wanted. And besides, I strongly suspected that she was beginning to suspect.

But on the way out we stopped at the main-floor lunch counter to have a snack, and I changed my whole outlook on whether the trip was worth-while. First, instead of the usual coke or ice cream, Laurie asked me very solemnly what I was having. When I said, "A cup of tea," she decided that was her choice, too. Then I noticed how very, very quiet she was, just sitting and watching, drinking in all the glitter and twinkling lights, the carols from the public-address system, and that wonderful heady perfume that floats on the air of all large department stores at Christmas.

We sat there quietly, sipping our tea, while Laurie made little grown-up observations now and then, and my feet began to hurt a fraction less, and gradually all the rush and confusion fell away from our little island of peace. Laurie was only six. It would seem that a woman-to-woman interlude like that would be beyond her understanding, wouldn't it? Yet when the other two greeted us at the door with breathless questions about Santa Claus, she said, "The part I really liked best was when we had tea together, just Mommy and me, and talked about things a little while."

Suddenly, just for one priceless instant, I had a glimpse into the future, a foretaste of the fun and companionship a mother-daughter relationship can offer when the daughter has grown to be a woman, too.

Many of my friends who are the mothers of both sons and daughters cite this adult closeness as one of the deepest joys of rearing little girls. No matter how stormy the period of adolescence, they find, there is always a drawing together again when a daughter marries and sets up a home of her own. All their adult lives a mother and daughter will speak the same language of home, family, children, woman talk. So universal is this experience that it has been incorporated in our folklore: "A son is a son till he gets him a wife; a daughter's a daughter for all of her life."

But this closeness is not found only in the later years. Right from the time—about their fourth or fifth year usually— when little boys begin to choose masculinity in their toys, interests, and friends, their mothers notice that there is a bond of understanding between mothers and little girls. It is not that we love our sons less, but simply that we remember. Little things—a Christmas doll, the evening sounds when children are playing under the street lights in the summer dusk, the scratchy, prickly feeling of an organdy slip—can suddenly cut through twenty years and suddenly we remember. We don't have to imagine what it's like to be a little girl; we know.

It is when we forget how it was, or when we begin to distrust the wisdom of our feminine instincts, that we falter.

Then we begin saying, "I just can't understand her!" But that's not true. Out of our own remembering, out of the years of living together, out of the love we bear her, in our hearts we understand. Our problem may be that we so often turn to the bookcase for an expert's answer, rather than sitting down in some quiet room and listening to the answer of our heart.

Recently there has been evidence of a popular revival of the custom of praying with our children. It's a pity we don't put equal emphasis on praying *for* our children. Whether your interpretation of prayer is the orthodox one, or whether you prefer to use the term "meditation," a few moments a day devoted to quiet, serious, prayerful thought about our daughters offers a fine start toward getting back to heart-instructed child rearing.

When we trust our instincts, we sense that each of our daughters needs something different from us. The mother of more than one daughter must be a sort of juggler of love. One little girl needs a quiet haven from the fears and anxieties that, for her, fill the world outside. Her sister needs a bright center for the rollicking friendships that are so necessary to her. One child thrives on good-humored teasing; another is crushed by the same raillery.

It is this difference in sensitivity that worries me about the current trend to make our children the butt of family jokes. Even when a child seems unhurt, can we really assess the terrible power of words? This "what monsters they are" attitude is funny, yes, as long as it isn't true. If it's true, then of course it isn't funny at all and chuckling over the situation surely isn't the answer. But even when it's only a habit, it's a dangerous habit to toy with.

When we focus so strongly on the hectic, chaotic aspects of family living; when we emphasize aggravation rather than contentment, confusion rather than order, we are subtly encouraging the very traits we claim we deplore. There is a phrase used in show business that applies to our children: he's beginning to believe his own publicity.

That happens to far too many mothers and their offspring. Recently four of us were sitting around a neighbor's table, drinking coffee and nibbling doughnuts, when we somehow got on the subject of the flu. Asiatic, occidental, all varieties. We had all been down with one type or another that winter, and we were regaling each other with the wealth of serio-comic anecdotes our children's antics during the crisis had provided. In the midst of our heavy humor I suddenly realized that what I remembered best were not the incidents for which I could cheerfully have throttled my girls at the time. No, what really stood out from that fever-ridden nightmare was, as usual, a nice, warm, sentimental incident. So I took a deep breath and, half expecting scorn, told the other women.

One afternoon Lindy had slipped into the bedroom, and to cheer me while I was ill, had slid a white square of cardboard into my hand, a homemade report card, charting her opinion of my rating as a mother.

COOKING—A

SOING—A

LOVING—A

IRNING—A

she had printed with infinite care. (Cleaning, my weakest spot, she had left ungraded with a tact and diplomacy that struck me as amazing in one so young.)

Well, for several minutes a silence hung over the coffee cups, then everyone started talking at once.

"They *can* be awfully sweet, can't they?"

"You know, Joanny did something yesterday that I thought was sort of cute. . . ."

"I complain a lot about Sharon, but really she's not a bad little girl. . . ."

Once begun, accounts of dozens of incidents came to light, all in a happy vein. In fact, once begun, an intriguing change of key occurred in our coffee-cup conversations. Instead of talking *down*, we began talking (and thinking) constructively. And once we changed our emphasis we discovered that we were all doing a far better job as mothers than we had given ourselves credit for.

As a matter of fact, when we began to compare notes instead of laments, we produced a regular clearinghouse of ideas that would have done justice to a panel of child psychologists. Here is the cream of just one week's exchange:

Idea. Most tattling springs from the good child's longing to do the forbidden thing she reports. "He did? Well, I'm glad I can trust you never to do such a thing!" is all the comment she needs. Substitute praise for action and tattling suddenly ceases to be a problem.

Idea. Announce plans for a party (or any such exciting project) to your very young children at the last possible moment. It's those days of breathless anticipation that bring keyed-up nerves, irritability, and even upset tummies. (Our town's wisest kindergarten teacher taught us that gem of wisdom!)

Idea. Bedwetting a problem? One girl's pediatrician suggests taking the child to the bathroom just before you go to bed, preferably about midnight. Keep this up until she stays dry for several nights, then advance the time a half-hour, to eleven thirty. When she is again dry, make your pilgrimage at eleven and so on, until you reach her regular bedtime. Be sure she's wide awake—sponge her face with a cool washcloth if necessary. (This worked like magic for some of us, not at all for others.)

Idea. In a suburban area where all the children seem to be little ones, even an eight or nine-year-old neighbor as a babysitter can offer you a great deal of freedom. The only difference is that you, of course, stay in the house. But your "mother's helper" can read to the children, or supervise their play while you catch up with your dressmaking or relax with a magazine or do your nails. Talk over her "fee" (which should be very small) with your helper's mother to be sure it's not out of line with her allowance.

Idea. Around the Easter and Christmas holidays plan the

children's meals to offset the amount of "junk" they'll consume. Substitute fruit for richer desserts, serve toast unadorned by jams, avoid pancakes or waffles with their accompanying syrup—in short, plan the blandest possible combinations.

Idea. No less an authority than Dr. Gesell discovered this: when the day arrives when one particular trait of your child simply cannot be borne another hour, when something *must* be done, then within five days she will go on to another phase without any action on your part. Why? I have no idea. But it's true. See if it isn't.

Idea. Don't be the villain when you can shift the responsibility to an inanimate object. The children are to come in these summer nights, not when you call them, but when the street lights come on. They wear snow pants when the porch thermometer dips to 40, fill the wading pool only when it rises to 80. Can Lindy see the movie at the Colvin? We look it up in the *Parents'* magazine movie guide, with their judgment accepted as final. Oh, the arguments you can avoid!

And that's just one week! Every time we get together now, we come up with some new or constructive slant that makes this business of being a mother an adventure. Yet we are the same young women who once had admitted to the pleasant times with obvious reluctance and something akin to shame at our unaccustomed show of tenderness. (Though any one of us would gladly have laid down her life for her child, I know.)

Is it any wonder that our children are not always sure where they stand with us? We are so aware of our love for them, so conscious that our love dictates every decision we make, every step we take. But children do not always recognize love when it has been translated into new shoes or piano lessons. They need to be *told*.

Daughters, especially, need to be told. Words are not enough, but words they must have. How else will they themselves learn to use words—warm words, loving words—without shame? If we want our daughters to be warm and loving women, they need to learn this. They need to be told that all we do for them we do out of love. Happily, little girls will accept this show of affection from their mothers longer than will little boys, and I intend to take advantage of my daughters' loving natures. I am going to take a stand!

More tender words, more loving words, more pleasant memories. For only the warm memories are worthy of heart room.

I'm going to hold my head high and admit that my children (except for that dreadful hour just before dinner) are thoroughly nice youngsters; that my husband (once we've both had breakfast) is pretty close to perfect; and that our home (except on washday or when we're expecting guests for dinner) is as peaceful and sunny a haven as I could wish.

Let's start a new fad. Let's stop being ashamed of honest tenderness. It may mean that we'll all be drummed out of the P.T.A. or never invited to share another cup of coffee in our neighbors' kitchens, but next time someone says, "Such sweet girls," let's look them right in the eye and answer firmly, "Yes, they are."

Even if our children are within earshot, let's come right out and say it.

In fact, if our children are within earshot, we might go all the way, and add—without apology—"We love them and we're proud of them; proud of the girls they are today, and proud of the women they are fast becoming!"

CHAPTER 15

How to Help Your
Daughter Marry Money

Iт's quite as easy to fall in love with a rich man as a poor one,
I've always heard. I can't confirm that from personal experience, but when I compare my husband with the husbands of
some of my friends who chose with their heads I can only
conclude that the heart is wiser.

Fortunately, though, for the peace of mind of mothers,
whether or not our daughters "marry money" doesn't depend
entirely on the man they marry. It's up to us, their mothers.
All of us know at least two families with about the same income and about the same demands upon that income, yet one
family is serenely solvent, the other harassed and striving and
forever in debt. The difference lies not in income but in outgo.
And intelligent handling of the outgo requires at least one
good manager on the team. Just in case she marries a man who

208

is overly casual about money, each of us can make sure our daughter has money-sense enough for two.

My mother so often quoted the Scotch proverb, "A woman can throw out more with a teaspoon than a man can bring home with a wheelbarrow." How true! But the good manager doesn't come by her thrift all in a moment when the organist plays the Recessional. So we're right back to those years of childhood training.

You started building a dowry for your daughter when you handed her first allowance to her and helped her work out a sensible spending plan for it, when you went with her to open her first savings account. No matter what age your daughter is today, *today* is the right time to give her gradually increasing responsibility for the family finances.

Even a toddler can be taught the value of turning off lights that aren't being used, closing the hall door to keep in the heat, placing the soap back in the soapdish after every use. When you are marketing, she can hand you items that you select from the shelves, because they are the best buys; when you get back home she can stack the canned goods in the cupboard in the most efficient way, put the teabags in the canister, empty the potatoes into the vegetable bin which will help to keep them fresh. All this will save you some time and effort; more important, your little helper is learning thrifty habits of "housemanship" and of careful purchase and storage of foodstuffs.

A four- or five-year-old can help work out a budget for a shopping trip downtown with you: so much for bus fare or parking fee, so much for the blouse you intend to buy for her, perhaps a little extra for ice cream or a coke.

Six is not a bit too early for her to take some part in the purchasing of her clothes. When you shop for her, take her with you; explain to her that this slip is Sanforized and that's why you chose it; that because this dress is wash-and-wear she will be able to wear it oftener; that stretch socks last longer than regular fitted socks. In a crowded store this takes infinite patience. Perhaps you'll find that a more practical solution is the mail-order catalogue. For some reason many women still associate a catalogue with the Mother Hubbard and the plow, and when they comment on a particularly becoming, frilly party dress, and are told it was bought from a mail-order house, they are always surprised. But hundreds of thousands of women shop this way, and the mail-order catalogues offer mothers of little girls a style-school de luxe. Here is all the information (thread count, type of fabric, washability, width of hem) that she needs to compare values.

Even if you still prefer to buy many of her clothes where you can try them on her first, an evening spent together over the catalogue can yield a very accurate idea of how much to allow for this and how much to allow for that. Which, of course, is all that a budget means. And the little girl who learns to cope with a budget at six will be a whiz at canny purchasing by the time she's twenty-six.

At seven she should be old enough to buy some of her own clothes. No, I'm *not* out of my mind. Seven is not one bit too soon to learn that socks costing twenty cents less will wear out sooner or creep down in back. It's not too soon to find out that the pretty panties with the ruffled elastic legs aren't nearly so comfortable as those plain ones at the same price probably would have been, or that a white blouse goes with every skirt and can be bleached if a highly dyed frozen sherbet stick drips down the front of it. And there's only one way to *really* find these things out, and that's to go ahead and make mistakes.

An eight-year-old should be doing a considerable part of your weekly marketing, not just run-to-the-store-and-get-me-a-loaf-of-bread errands, but trips that involve decisions. ("If the rye bread doesn't seem truly fresh, get rolls instead." "Bring a head of lettuce, too, and if the heads are very small, bring two." "Use your own judgment.")

We have a delicatessen on the corner and a supermarket a block and a half away. Our girls learned young that by walking that extra block and a half they could save a little something on many purchases. They learned it because, if they were willing to walk to the supermarket and save me a few cents, they got to keep one penny for themselves. Now, at the sophisticated ages of eight and ten, a penny is no longer a dazzling fortune, but the habit persists and the pennies count up. On the other hand, they've learned that not all values can be measured in dollars and cents. If it's raining or if we're holding dinner for an item, they'll pay a little more at the smaller store. Sometimes they'll buy there just because of the nice, warm, personal feeling a neighborhood store exudes, but they're growing up with the knowledge that the friendly pat on the head and the free licorice whip are indirectly added onto the bill, a lesson many an inexperienced bride has had to learn the expensive way.

A mother can encourage the school-age girl to use her newly discovered mathematical prowess to compare prices and ounces.

You can give her a set amount of money to cover a birthday party and let her decide for herself how it's to be spent. When the whole family goes to an amusement park for an afternoon, it would be good training to give your older girls as much money as you intend to spend on them, and let them make the decisions as to how much shall go for tickets for the rides, how much to save out for the refreshment stand. The same system can apply on vacation trips, for souvenir buying.

All this takes patience and time and a great deal of self-control. For when we say, "Use your own judgment," then we can't scold or sneer when her judgment is wrong; we can only point out why we would have done it differently. It would certainly be easier to dispatch all these little financial decisions with a quick adult hand. But by giving her a chance to *use* money, we are building a daughter's dowry. She is developing a built-in sense of money management that will be worth more to her when she's on her own than a sock full of money would be.

And the older they get, the more we can do. I have noted with great interest the growing trend, among our friends who have teenage children, toward giving their youngsters real responsibility for the family budget.

In one family the fifteen-year-old son is responsible for keeping records of all monthly and quarterly bills—insurance premiums, payments on the mortgage and the car, everything—and making out a check for each which he presents to his Dad for signing, and then mails.

In another family every girl (and there are six!) buys all her own clothes after she reaches her thirteenth birthday. Yes, they've made some serio-comic mistakes, but only at thirteen and fourteen; by the time they are in high school these are really mature young shoppers. Their mother presents each girl with a copy of *Your Clothing Dollar,* another of those invaluable Household Finance booklets, at the beginning of that first buying year.

One irate father of my acquaintance who has a daughter in college survived one semester of frantic wires and letters for more money and then put his foot down. During midterm vacation he asked her to make a list of her anticipated needs and arrive at an over-all figure, then he handed her a check for that amount and a round-trip train ticket.

"This," he announced, "is it. There will be no more, even in the direst emergency."

She had estimated far too low, of course, failing to allow for all sorts of unforeseen expenses; it was a semester she's not likely to forget. But the sophomore year worked out well, and in her junior year she ended up with a few dollars in the bank. This year, her Dad tells me, she asked him for the train-fare money instead of the ticket, explaining that she'll ride a bus and bank the difference.

A most dramatic case of giving the adolescent a free hand with the purse strings came about because the children of two couples we know fell in love. Both sets of parents felt vaguely that their children were too young, but since Shirley had a fairly good job and Phil had only one more year of college, and since they were so obviously right for each other in every way, the families had no intention of barring their way. In fact, it was with the idea of helping that Phil's father arranged to have him take over the household budget for several months. His idea was that this is training a man about to found a family of his own should have.

About the same time Shirley asked her parents if she could do the marketing and some of the cooking, a sort of last-minute cramming session. Now these were two intelligent young people who honestly believed that they understood what it took to operate a household, but after two months of actually operating their respective homes they decided—all on their own—to postpone the wedding until Phil had his degree and a job. The experiment would be equally eye-opening if it were undertaken with just that result in mind!

Just the harsh realities of holding a job (even a summer job or a paper route or a baby-sitting business) will teach a daughter much about the years ahead. Every girl should have some experience in the business world before she marries, no matter how early. She'll be a more serene and secure wife if she knows she can support her little brood in a crisis. But outgo is as important as income ("A woman can throw out more with a teaspoon...") and she needs to grow gradually into the ability to spend money as well as to earn it.

Earlier this year I entered the Mrs. America contest, and though I got no farther than competing in the state finals, I did win the title of "Mrs. Buffalo" and all the thrilling prizes that the title carries. Equally exciting has been the aftermath

—a chain of exciting interviews and radio and television appearances. All this is simply to explain how it came about that Harriet Cooke, the food editor of our local paper, wrote a column around my pet ideas about spending food money so you save it.

Mrs. Cooke's article brought me more letters and phone calls than any other publicity did. A few women were frankly skeptical about the paragraph that said I feed all five of us on a total household budget of $22.00 a week, but most of the women who wrote or called were enthusiastic and interested. Either they were holding down costs and wanted to share their favorite thrift tricks with me or they were spending more than they felt they should and wanted to add a few more short cuts to their repertoire. One of the most revealing facts was that many of the readers who got in touch with me were older women who had passed the grim-economy phase of their lives. Their husbands had risen in their businesses or professions, and among such women I found that a food budget of $50.00 to $60.00 a week was not considered extravagant. Yet all these older women expressed the same concern—how to prepare their daughters for the frugal buying and careful planning usually so necessary during the first years of marriage. Apparently most women want to be efficient purchasing agents and homemakers. They want to raise their children to be even better managers than they are.

How does one go about it? Well, this is what I am teaching the daughters at our house:

Our greatest savings come from shopping from a list, with a week's menus made up in advance. And I *stick to that list!* The men who keep track of such things tell us that fewer than one out of three shoppers ever go to the trouble of preparing a shopping list, and that's a pity, for an accurate list is essential to efficient marketing. And efficient marketing is the first of the Three Basic Steps toward thrift in homemaking. The Basic Three are:

1. Careful marketing
2. Planned storage and preparation
3. Imaginative serving

But to get back to the marketing, I sit down each Thursday evening with the newspaper ads, a pencil, my big manila envelope of recipes and menu ideas, and a long sheet of tablet paper. Down one side I list the days of the week, then choose the main dish for each day, using the specials in the ads as a guide. This is where the girls often like to help, suggesting dishes we've neglected too long, or the favorites of which they never tire. They know that I allow a certain amount a week for meat, so if they want beef or lamb at one meal, they know they must balance that with franks-and-beans another night, or with a soup-and-salad or soup-and-hearty-sandwich meal if it's summer.

The girls check the cupboard for staples that are getting low, and I add to the list the ingredients we'll need for the meals we've planned. Here's how this week's list looked when we were through:

Thursday
Hamburger patties
Mashed potatoes
Vegetable
   Pie (Lemon meringue)

Friday
Swiss steak
Baked potatoes
   Salad
     Cookies

Saturday
Spaghetti
Chef's salad, garlic bread
   Cookies and fruit

Hamburger—3½ pounds
Chuck—1 pound
Lunch meat
Margarine, cheese, bread
Flour
Corn meal, oatmeal
Sugar, granulated and brown
Stew—2 cans
Tuna—2
Fruit juice
Corn
Frenched beans
Baked beans—2
Apricots

Sunday
Individual meat loaves
Hurry-up potatoes
Corn, head lettuce
  Gingerbread

Monday
Tomato soup
Tuna salad, muffins
  Chocolate cake

Tuesday
Macaroni and cheese
Tossed salad, cranberries
  ambrosia and cookies

Wednesday
Beef 'n' beans
Fruit salad, Boston brown
    bread
Chocolate cake

Soup—3
Gingerbread mix
Macaroni
Cocoa
Lettuce, tomatoes, cucumber
Potatoes, cranberries
Bananas, lemons
Waxed paper
Paper towels

This meal-planning session is a perfect setting for introducing the children to a few pertinent facts about homemaking.

We have a nutrition chart, for example, a big wheel with all the essential food elements listed, and the girls check the meals against the chart and delight in catching me up on something I've forgotten.

Some of our favorite food ideas have originated with the children. Breakfast-in-a-glass (an egg beaten into a glass of orange juice) was Lindy's invention. So were bacon buns (just leftover hot-dog buns served for breakfast the next morning filled with crisp bacon strips). And it was Laurie who started our family fad for faces. We put faces on everything—raisin faces on the oatmeal, carrot-slice faces on the cottage cheese, even faces formed from cranberries on the mashed potatoes.

I hope Lindy and Laurie are learning something else during our frequent huddles over the menus. I hope they are learning that economizing can take on the challenge of a hobby, if we refuse to feel sorry for ourselves. Anyone can be a good cook with expensive cuts of meat, vegetables bathed in butter, gravy rich with real cream. But the true sense of accomplishment—and this is the philosophy I hope the girls will absorb—comes of making our meals so tasty and so attractive that only the cook knows the careful planning it took to make ends meet.

One of our pet economies is to buy reconstituted powdered milk which we mix half and half with water and whole milk for drinking, and to buy canned milk for cooking and baking. Also, we're frugal about buying prepared foods, which are always more expensive than the same dish cooked "from scratch." Pie-filling mixes, for instance, save roughly four minutes in preparation time but cost nearly 75 per cent more than the individual ingredients.

But careful buying is only one third of the question: Storing and preparation is the second responsibility. And here's where the waste mounts up. How many times I've let a sack of onions or potatoes get pushed to the back of the cupboard, finding it only when the smell reminded us! Or how many little jars of leftovers finally are thrown out on defrosting day, dried out or moldy.

The savings we can pocket through proper careful storage and preparation are penny small. Thin peelings, so little cooking water that few vitamins are lost, a stock jar for vegetable liquors, a can for bacon drippings, a paper towel lining the crisper to cut down on spoilage, each of these will save very little, but surely I don't have to quote Benjamin Franklin's "a penny saved," to convince you about small savings. ("A woman can throw out more with a teaspoon . . .")

But these are the savings that take habit, that you have to

train your girls to remember. The thrift that is really fun comes in the serving.

The greatest single weapon a woman wields in her battle to feed the family well on what she has to spend is appearance.

The appearance of the food itself—color selection, arrangement on the plate, garnish—all these are important. Important, too, is the flair for glamour or clever novelty you manage to impart to every meal.

For instance, when a meal is very obviously budget fare, I always try to add some one thing the family considers a treat— hot biscuits, or a gelatin salad, or perhaps just chocolate milk instead of plain. Herbs, parsley, mint, and chives (even a window box is big enough to grow all four) also give a lift to any meal, not just by the extra fillip of flavor, but as an attractive garnish.

I find that our girls react very strongly to the name of a new dish, and a sense of drama in titling your creations makes all the difference in how they are accepted. We never have stew or hash at our house. Or, rather, we never have a dish called stew or hash. But Mystery Casserole and Persian Blend are real favorites. They consider they're eating like royalty when I serve Crown Roast of Frankfurters, too, which is probably the cheapest company meal in the world. I string hot dogs on a length of heavy string through the middle and again at one end, tie the strings so that the franks will stand on end like a crown roast. The girls then fill the middle with seasoned mashed potatoes and we pop it in the oven to heat through. Our three girls are learning that even leftovers can be good eating. When we have dibs and dabs of main dishes left over, I put them in little foil pie plates (though custard cups would do as well) and freeze them. Then one night I put all the little pans on a cookie sheet and slide them into the oven to warm. I plan a nice salad and a special dessert and line all the pans up in a row on the buffet and let everyone choose her own. They've dubbed this a Cafeteria Dinner and consider it quite a treat.

But it's not tricks that I hope to pass on to our daughters—but a philosophy—my own deep conviction that economy needn't be dreary. Eating well requires time, money, and effort, but we can juggle the proportion of each of those three ingredients. If we haven't much money, we simply make up the difference with more time and more effort.

Some of that effort invested in stage-setting the meal will yield handsome dividends. The principles of Beauty All Around Her applies to dining rooms, too! The most delicious meal loses something if it's served in the kitchen, with the bread in its wrapper and the milk in the bottle. Or if it is served in a dark, drab dining room. With paint so inexpensive and colors so smart today, there is no reason not to have a bright, attractive setting for any meal. Linen napkins, which many of us seldom use now that the paper ones come in such attractive styles and colors, can be ironed flat and used as table mats, old cloths can be tinted to look new and fresh, plants from the window sill can become centerpieces—there's just no end to the ways in which a table can be given an exciting new look. And no one can tell me that all this costs money, for just six months ago the winning table setting I arranged for the New York State finals of the Mrs. America Contest (and which was awarded the silver bowl for Imaginative Table Setting) consisted of a three-year-old rayon cloth, plastic dishes, "candlesticks" that were really dime-store ash trays, ten cents-plus-a-box-top salt and peppers, last year's straw purse, and a peanut-butter glass!

When it comes to wise money management of house-furnishings and clothes, the same three careful steps apply, with slightly altered labels:

> Purchasing
> Care
> Presentation

Clothes are easier, when it comes to early training, because the wise mother—as I've said before—starts her female off-spring off young on the purchasing angle. Then this wise mother either teaches her daughter to sew or encourages her to enroll in a sewing course, not only so that she can make her own clothes, but so that she can care for them properly. For the most expensive clothes lose style unless they are faultlessly maintained and groomed, and the least expensive clothes need even more tender loving care if they are to look twice their price. Of course, that T. L. C. is tiresome, and it isn't easy to convince a teenager (unless she's dreaming of being a model) that it's worth the effort. Again, as with food thrift, so much depends on good habits, instilled early. It was for this that we have asked our girls for years to hang up their coats and to tidy their dresser drawers. We can do more than that while they are young, though. As our daughters enter that pre-teen no-woman's-land of gift giving where they are too old for dolls and too young for cosmetics, they usually cherish glamorous grooming accessories of all kinds: a full-length mirror, or a pretty quilted fitted mending box of their own. Or a completely renovated clothes closet. After you have papered or painted the closet walls, added scalloped shelf edg-ing, colorful garment bags, satin-covered hangers with sachet, hatbox, shoe bag equipped with whisk broom, shoe trees, and suède brush, all in beautifully harmonized shades, any little girl will take clothes care more seriously.

But let's not lose sight of the fact that this little girl will someday be a wife, with more than her own wardrobe to care for. You can start her young checking pockets and cuffs before she takes her dad's suit to the cleaner's. You can teach her the facts of life about wool overcoats and moths. And even if you customarily send your husband's shirts to the laundry, in this land where 67 per cent of all business shirts are laun-dered at home, it might be wise to think in terms of that future son-in-law, and schedule two solid sessions at the ironing board—one to teach her how to iron a shirt, one to teach her how to press a suit. That's marriage training she'll bless you for in years to come.

Presentation? Why, that's the way the clothes are "served up," and the same flair for color and proportion, for drama, for accessorizing, that makes for memorable meals will help your daughter look her best. Her father can help by impressing on this future bride the importance of a man's appearance as a legitimate business expense. In too many homes Dad's clothes money is what's left over when all other expenses are taken care of. In very, very few homes does the budget provide the $225 a year that fashion authorities have estimated as a minimum replacement cost to keep a man's wardrobe adequate to the demands of a white-collar job.

Later, when your daughter is shopping for and maintaining a wardrobe for two, and then for three or more, all this groundwork will be just like money in the bank.

While the sums involved in furniture preclude youthful experiments, there's a lot you can teach your little girl about furnishings just the same.

It's her home, too, and from her very, very early years she should have some say in every new purchase or rearrangement of furniture. If she doesn't, if the house is your showplace, you can hardly complain when in her teens she shows no interest, and certainly no pride, in its upkeep.

Sometimes a mother will plan for years that one day she'll have enough money to do over her daughter's bedroom, while year by year the room grows more faded and drab. When that happens, it's time to lower our standards and settle happily for half a loaf. It's fabulous what one energetic teenager can do with even ten or fifteen dollars and a scrapbook of dream-room clippings and a free rein.

Even without a penny's expenditure we can initiate our girls into the mysteries of Care and Maintenance. In fact, a great deal of it can be turned over to them completely. Daughters love to devise and keep up a filing system for instructions, guarantees, washing directions, etc. And in this day of do-it-yourself even the most feminine of daughters may be taught to replace an electric plug, or refinish a table, or shampoo a rug.

And just think, all the time you are encouraging your daughter in these housewifely pursuits you are building up to the day when the vice-president's wife will murmur to her husband, "Young Jones is just the man for the job, dear. That wife of his —so clever, so artistic, such a good manager!"

John L. Handy, a management consultant recently contributing to a magazine symposium on how to achieve solvency and security, ended his advice with this observation, which sums up neatly the role for which we are preparing our daughters:

"For the young man on his way up," advises Mr. Handy, *"the biggest single blessing is a saving wife."*

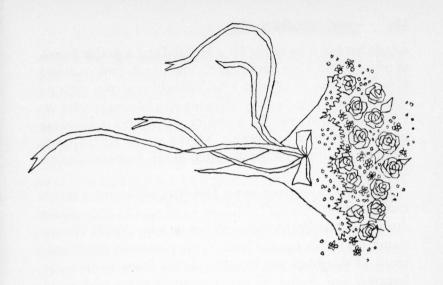

CHAPTER 16

You Are Molding Her Marriage Today

IT's always a little sad—a father's dream for his son to follow in his footsteps. And what father doesn't dream of it, whatever the vocational counselors may warn? The new shingle swinging below the weathered one beside the office door. The little store on a side street, its sign repainted to proclaim "... *and son.*" But it's sad, because so very often the dream is doomed. For every son who joins the firm there are a dozen who break their fathers' hearts. And that it's right and wise and necessary for them to do this makes it no less tragic.

But mothers are luckier; our daughters all come "into the business," if we are wise enough to see our business as the whole broad scope of homemaking. Whether a daughter spends her full time caring for a husband and a sizable brood, or whips through her family chores and joys in time snatched from her career, or chooses a bachelor-girl existence with no activity more domestic than whipping up a late-night snack on a hot plate, so long as she is making a home she is following in the tradition of her mother. So you see we have only to interpret our dream for our daughters loosely to see our dreams come true.

To follow in our own career footsteps, to become a junior member of the firm, isn't that how we all see it? One woman's dream may take the form of a kitchen on some distant Thanksgiving, a kitchen fragrant and buzzing with the last-minute bustle of daughters and daughters-in-law home for the day. Laughter and chatter fill that visionary kitchen, and grandchildren race about forever underfoot.

My own personal dream tends toward a cottage by the ocean, where married daughters and their handsome husbands people the beaches, while beautiful bronze grandchildren clamber about on the rocks.

However unsentimental you may claim to be, you have one, too—that mental picture of your daughter grown. A fine woman you want her to be, and a happy woman. Talented, too, perhaps, especially if you have a shining talent of your own. But most of all—and let us state it baldly and without shame—most of all you hope for your daughter, from the day of her birth, a good marriage.

It's up to you, the kind of man who'll appeal to her.

To a girl who is miserable at home, any male who offers a strong shoulder and a sympathetic ear will look like Prince Charming. But a happy, well-adjusted teenager must be very, very sure of her love to overcome that natural reluctance to leave the good world of home.

Erich Fromm, who is a psychoanalyst of note as well as a

writer of great skill, has produced a slim volume of wisdom called *The Art of Loving,* one of the beautifully done *World Perspective* series published by Harper's. Admittedly, it is not a book for browsing or skimming at the end of a hard day. But it's worth every bit of mental effort it requires. This is a book quite useless, I should think, to a young girl in love, but a book that her mother will understand and cherish. You may want to read it for yourself; however, one point that Mr. Fromm makes bears directly on this question of selecting a mate.

He points out that one of the most delightful manifestations of this thing we call love is the sudden sensation of oneness with another human being. But to a lonely young woman who has felt shut off, isolated all her life, this pleasant sensation comes as a dazzling miracle. Caught up in the wonder of being loved for the first time, nothing else matters. But a girl who has been surrounded with love from her crib days can better retain her sense of perspective. That happy child will take longer to mull over all the consequences of early marriage, and will be more apt to wait until the right time, as well as the right man, comes along. So the first obvious step toward assuring her happy marriage is to give your daughter a happy home.

If a little girl grows up loving her father, she will nearly always make a wiser choice of a mate than girls who fear or dislike or have contempt for their fathers. And it's been proved again and again that little girls who grow up without a father or feeling rejected by the one they have wander about all their lives, looking for that father they missed. Inevitably that search leads them into attachments with older men. Too great an age difference is a threat to the success of her marriage, of course; a greater threat to her happiness is that so few of the men she'll meet in the gray-at-the-temples set will be eligible for marriage. But by giving her a father, by encouraging her to have a nor-

mally close, happy relationship, you'll have pointed her tastes
in the direction of boys her own age.

Not that we can leave the age matter all up to her taste.
That's one rule a mother is wise to enforce vigorously—that her
child must date within her own general age group.

That is, however, about the only group we can limit her to.
The days when a girl was advised to date boys "of her own
kind" disappeared when Americans began to migrate in great
surging waves out of the city, with its sharply defined neighborhoods, into the suburbs. Here, where the plumber, the professor, the young bank executive, and the fight promoter all live
on the same street, bowl in the same league, and send their
sons to the same college, who is "her own kind"?

In these days there's very little chance that your daughter
will marry a boy she's known all her life, whose parents have
been your friends for years, whose ways are all your ways. She
will almost surely marry a boy who has lived in parts of our
country that she has never glimpsed; if so, even though his
economic and social status may be exactly the same as your
own, his standards of dress, his speech, his political ideas, even
his taste in foods, will reflect his different background. In this
sense, most marriages are "mixed marriages" today. Indeed, a
young couple of different nationality and religion who have
grown up together in the same community may find fewer
points of conflict than a couple who are carefully matched as
to externals but whose dreams and goals and ideals are far
apart.

Yet we mothers still dread the thought of our daughters
marrying someone "different." Is it snobbishness? I think not.
I believe that we sense what every bride in a mixed marriage
soon learns, that in building a new family a young couple will
both drift away from the old ways of their parents toward common ground. They must, if they are to build a strong new
family unit of their own. But it's hard on mothers, for we then
feel that our daughters have left us behind.

In a sense they have. Stephen Vincent Benét, in *Western Star*, the monumental narrative poem of our American heritage which was left unfinished at his death, said of our English ancestors landing in America:

> And those who came were resolved to be Englishmen,
> Gone to the world's end, but English every one,
> And they ate the white corn kernels, parched in the sun,
> And they knew it not, but they'd not be English again.*

As our daughters learn to cook with olive oil or chicken fat or fat back, as they murmur to our grandchildren a nickname or an endearment in a language strange to our ears, we fear we have lost them.

And so we may, unless we change within ourselves. If we bridle at every foreign phase of their lives, we build up tensions and defenses that will make them uncomfortable in our presence. Gradually they will arrange to see less of us, or at least will not look forward to our visits to their homes or their visits to ours.

But if we can accept new blood into our family with enthusiasm, if we can admit that our ways are not the only ways, are not even necessarily better, then we can smoothe the path before this fragile new marriage.

A mixed marriage (of any combination of differences) has a few more hurdles to vault than any homogeneous marriage. And the loving, understanding, and unquestioning acceptance of even one pair of sensible parents can be just the extra boost the marriage needs.

Such differences in customs and rituals are far less important than differences in character and ideals, aren't they? And if you have raised a fine young woman with a high standard of loving, you can rest assured that, so far as character is con-

---

* From *Western Star* by Stephen Vincent Benét, Rinehart & Company, Inc. Copyright 1943 by Rosemary Carr Benét.

cerned, she'll eventually choose "her own kind"—in terms of character and ethics—to marry.

It's up to you, the kind of man she'll attract.
Some chapters back we devoted pages and pages to beauty, remember? Well, here's where it all pays off in a lifetime of happiness. If you have taught her to choose clothes to enhance her type, if her training in grooming began when you first helped her lay out just the right socks and hair ribbons for each day at kindergarten, if she is well read and well informed, if she has the poise, the gentle manners, the indefinable aura of a lady, she will have the boys beating a path to her door.

If she *knows* she's lovely, if you have given her the confidence bred of acceptance just as she is, then she will be able to marry just about any many her heart chooses.

There's a bigger stake involved than just whether or not she'll make a good marriage. A girl's opinion of herself dictates the price she sets on herself before marriage.

That's another of those nagging worries that plague mothers but that are too frightening to voice. Or it was too frightening to voice until recently; lately we hear and read a great deal about chastity—and about its opposite—among today's teens. But it seems to me that much of this voluminous literature on youthful morality misses the point. It misses the point because it puts all the emphasis on virginity. And virginity is a negative virtue.

Now *there's* a statement guaranteed to raise eyebrows! But it's not the amoral theory it may seem on the surface. The point is that we don't say, "My daughter is honest—she has never robbed a bank," or, "My daughter is gentle—she doesn't beat her dog." We are all aware that the first girl may still be thoroughly dishonest and the second girl harsh and cruel. It's equally ridiculous oversimplification to say that because a girl has stopped short of the final commitment she is consequently chaste.

In short, virginity is not enough. A girl may be a cheap, vulgar, boy-chasing little tramp and still be technically a virgin, but that will be small comfort to her disappointed parents. The Girl Scout laws face up to this problem squarely: A Girl Scout is pure in thought, word, and deed.

And that's our goal, isn't it? We want daughters who are so wholesome and healthy minded, so busy with a multitude of sports and hobbies and enthusiasm, so self-disciplined and sensible, that sex satisfaction takes it rightful place in a happy and secure future.

I spent my first four school years in a Catholic convent school, where all of us—non-Catholics, too—were expected to commit such basic tenets as the Smaller Catechism and the Ten Commandments to memory. I can remember so clearly the day when Lizzie Johnson, from whom most of us had already learned the fundamental facts of life, asked what "Thou shalt not commit adultery" meant. I remember how uncomfortable Sister Richards looked, and how she stared at a spot just above the back blackboard as she answered that adultery meant gluttony or greed. I remember, too, that we giggled behind our hands.

But how right that good woman was! Chastity becomes a problem largely for the demanding, greedy child who has learned to snatch what she wants, when she wants it, regardless of whom she hurts. It is not farfetched to maintain that years of consistent, loving training in self-discipline, in love of beauty, in developing the warm, responsive insight of an educated heart, in duty and responsibility, in plain good manners, will have more effect on our daughters' morality than all the lectures we can deliver.

And it will have an effect on their beaus, too. Such a girl, by her very bearing and attitude, inspires a feeling of respect in the boys she dates. "A lady," as Russell Lynes said, "is a woman who makes a man behave like a gentleman."

Other steps we have taken through the years will bear fruit

now, too. All those childhood years when your attractive, hospitable home was the favorite place to play were a prelude to these teenage years, when your daughter and her gang are dancing in the basement instead of petting on Lookout Hill.

But the biggest contribution we can make to the defense of our daughters' morals is based on the age-old law of supply and demand. The really special girls, the ones blessed with looks, personality, character, and a realistic sense of their own worth have always been able to write their own tickets. These are the popular girls. These are the girls who don't have to make it worth-while for a boy to date them. Raised with love and common sense, yours can be one of the very special girls.

And raised with love and common sense, your daughter has all the preparation you can give her for selecting a lifetime mate. Now let her select him. If she hasn't found any man she wants, don't press her. There's a whole world of satisfaction and worth and value for the woman who never marries or for the woman who marries late in life. In fact, many a contented career woman wouldn't change anything about the life she lives—except the disappointed mother who keeps her forever on the defensive.

But if your daughter has found a man she's sure she loves, trust her. You can prepare her to make a clear-headed choice, but you can't choose for her. You should be honest; you can tell her, strong and straight and without mincing any words, if you honestly believe this man is wrong for her, or just wrong. But having had your say, trust her.

Trust her to choose wisely and trust her ability to bring out the best in the man she's chosen. Many a pimply-faced, tongue-tied boy has developed into a man of substance and stature through the alchemy of a perceptive woman's love. "What does she see in him?" we wonder. The answer is that she sees —often more accurately than we—the man he can become.

Robert Browning said it most romantically:

God be thanked, the meanest of his creatures
Boasts two soul-sides, one to face the world with,
One to show a woman when he loves her.

It's up to you how happy they'll be.

What this country's girl children need is less "Cinderella" and more "Frog Prince." Cinderellas don't really marry the Princes and that's-the-end-of-the-story. We get married to a man, just a man, a husband whose name and walk and grin are all familiar but who may turn out to be anyone at all underneath that outer shell. We marry him and then use all the love we possess to find the key that will break the spell. When we succeed, the Prince emerges. Our girls should be told about that.

They should be told that in every marriage ever solemnized there lies the seed of a great, soaring, storybook romance, if only they can find it and nourish it. They should be told that a good marriage grows better and better through the years, but that in the very early years it is fragile and easily damaged, that it must be sheltered like the tender shoots of a very young plant. They need to know that we—their mothers and fathers —are on their sides, that with all our hearts we want this marriage to succeed, that they can count on us to inspire and cheer and hearten them, to do nothing that will add stresses or pressures that might cause the delicate new marriage harm.

The American Institute of Family Relations offers a booklet called *How to Be a Good Mother-in-Law and Grandmother*, by Edith G. Neisser (25¢), that sets up a practical, immediate course of action. But once again you'll find the important steps were taken years and years ago.

The way you felt about your daughter's grandmother, for instance, will have left its mark on your child for good or ill and will largely determine the warmth of the relationship she'll work out with her mother-in-law.

The background you gave her, her home, her cultural standards, her manners, will largely determine the position she'll occupy in the hierarchy of her husband's family. Of course you don't want her to be an affected little snob; still, it will do her marriage no harm at all if her in-laws obviously think their son made a mighty lucky catch!

It's up to you whether she'll be a vital, dynamic, energetic wife. Remember all the vitamins, all the cod-liver oil you've administered through the years? You surely didn't dole them out to insure her eventual happy marriage. But that's just what you were doing. All those nature walks and swimming lessons and tennis-court fees and summer camps will make a contribution, too. For every group experienced in counseling has discovered the importance of a healthy wife in building a happy marriage. Many a marriage has been snatched back from the brink of divorce by a doctor's findings that anemia or a vitamin deficiency or near-breakdown exhaustion were beneath the slovenly housekeeping, waspish temper, sexual apathy, or fading looks that showed on the surface.

We can raise our daughters with a middle-of-the-road attitude toward illness, neither overanxious hypochondriacs nor stoics or martyrs who refuse to see a doctor when they need one. We can raise them to have a healthy respect for intelligent eating habits, ample sleep, exercise, fresh air.

That's only part of the general pride we must teach a daughter in her body and its functions. If you hail her first menstruation as an exciting milestone, a badge of her womanhood, if she knows you enjoyed your own pregnancies, and that you consider the birth of a baby a joyous miracle, if she senses throughout her childhood that you and her father cherish the intimate relationships of married love, she'll be off to a fine healthy start. Then, during the early years of her marriage, if you'll insist that she tell her health problems to her doctor instead of pouring her symptoms into your patient, sympathetic ear, you'll have finished the job. She will be well equipped for one of the most vital jobs of her new career: safeguarding the health of her children (with a sure knowledge of what is scientific and what is superstition) and the health of her husband (aware that a home that is an island of peace and comfort and calm is the best health insurance a husband can carry).

It's up to you whether she has fun on the job.

Why is it that mothers who wouldn't dream of consenting to their daughter's marrying a boy who was incapable of earning a living will, without compunction, saddle some unsuspecting lad with a bride who's utterly incapable of running a household? No matter how much the comics may chuckle over a bride's first biscuits, the situation is basically pathetic. And it's all your fault!

There's nothing smart about the mother who brags that her children have never had to lift a finger. And there's nothing cute about the woman, and she is supposed to be a woman, now that she's a wife, who can't turn out a taut bed, a high cake, or a white wash.

The girl who brings to marriage skill and competence in her household jobs has four advantages over the bungling novice:

1. She knows, and her new husband knows, that she is carrying her weight in the partnership, without apology or defensiveness. And self-confidence is a vital factor in any human relationship.

2. She impresses onlookers as a quick, bright girl. The bride who times all the foods in her meal to come out even, or whose housekeeping can take a drop-in visit from the boss's wife in her stride, reaps compliments for her superior ability, though it may be nothing but years of practice under her mother's tutelage. It's unfair, but—that's the nature of people!

3. She has so much more fun! Statistics indicate that your young lady will remain at her desk or her counter for awhile after the wedding. If keeping her shiny new apartment tidy and keeping her shiny new bridegroom fed are backbreaking,

time-consuming burdens, those first few months won't include any of the delightful recreation they both want and need.

How do we develop her skill and competence? My own ideas on that subject make up a dozen of the earlier chapters. But one additional theory I can't resist expounding here:

Exposure isn't enough. No matter how welcome our toddlers are in the kitchen, no matter how willingly they lend their hands to chores, they still require instruction. We spend hundreds of dollars for their lessons in music, swimming, riding. We mortgage the car to send them to business school. But when it comes to the job they will hold, at least part time, for the rest of their lives, we just turn 'em loose.

I'm afraid it's pride, partly. When I know how much work goes into a meal, it irritates me to have a blissfully ignorant grade-school child offer to "cook dinner." Because she's so sure there's nothing to it, it's a temptation to let her try it, and even to be a little smug about the fiasco. Petty? Of course, but I'll bet I'm not alone in that reaction.

We need to give or buy them actual lessons in each field. We need to provide them with an authoritative manual in each—a cookbook, a beginner's sewing book, one volume on home management. And then, while they are learning, we need to give them opportunity to practice, even if it would be easier and quicker ourselves.

When should this formal training begin? You'll sense it. Every girl comes to a day when she's bored with the primary level and coaxes to move up. That's the first trick—to catch her interest when the time is right.

The second trick is to start the lessons anywhere but at the bottom. That's why introducing her to homemaking skills very young is an advantage. Now all that routine is behind her. The ten-year-old girl wants to create a molded pressed-chicken loaf, not tuna salad, a dress to wear to school, not a pot holder or penwiper.

Another trick is to utilize puppy love. There is nothing like a starry-eyed interest in one particular boy to stimulate her interest in all the feminine skills. But you'll discover other tricks, and invent a few of your own.

The end result will be the same: a married daughter who can take the drudgery of housework in her stride, leaving time and energy for the more rewarding tasks. That girl will handle all the demands of her new status with casual good humor.

And that would be the greatest gift of all—casual good humor—except that unfortunately it cannot be given; each of us must find it for herself. But we can give her every help by encouraging the lighthearted approach to life whenever she exhibits it. The relaxed, serene wife who can laugh at mishaps, who takes neither others nor herself too seriously, is a joy to her family and to everyone she meets. Indeed, if all the traits and skills necessary to a happy marriage were compiled, surely a wife's sunny disposition would head the list.

Never complain because wives are expected to do so much of the adapting in marriage. Never complain that the bulk of marriage improvement is directed to women. Instead, be forever grateful that now, as always, most of the weight of building a strong marriage falls on the wife. For don't you see? If we turn out a daughter who is a superb wife, she can scarcely fail to build a good marriage, even with the most unfortunate choice of mate.

But if we turn out a daughter who is a superb wife, and who is also able to attract and to appreciate a superb husband, what wings we've given her for all her life!

These May Help

CHAPTER 2

Pounds and Personality, by Dr. Gladys Andrews of New York University, available without charge from "Chubbette," Dept. RD, Middlesex, New Jersey.

Beauty Book for Beginners, excellent basic beauty plan, available from Good Housekeeping Bulletin Service, 57th Street at Eighth Avenue, New York 19, New York (10¢ in stamps).

CHAPTER 3

Decorating Is Fun, by Dorothy Draper, published by Doubleday & Company, Inc., New York, New York.

McCall's Book of Family Manners, a thirty-six-page booklet of wonderfully down-to-earth rules for daily living and for special occasions, too. Write to McCall's Modern Homemaker, Post Office Box 1390, Grand Central Station, New York 17, New York (25¢ in coin).

American Heritage, 551 Fifth Avenue, New York 17, New York.

The American Art Directory, published annually by R. R. Bowker Co., 62 West 45th Street, New York 36, New York, and available at most libraries, provides the most up-to-date information. Most large art museums provide some or all of the services mentioned in Chapter 3, but policies vary from year to year.

Great Books of the Western World, 425 North Michigan Avenue, Chicago 11, Illinois.